FILE FOLDER
LEARNING
CENTERS

for Bible Study Fun

by Donna Skinner

STANDARD PUBLISHING
Cincinnati, Ohio   3071

Scripture quotations are from these versions: the *King James, The New International,* © 1973 by New York Bible Society International, and *The Living Bible,* © 1971 by Tyndale House Publishers. Both are used by permission.

Dedicated to my family: Jesus, Don, Shōna, Kathryn, and David

illustrators: John Ham, Steve Hayes, and Ned Ostendorf

ISBN: 0-87239-492-1

Library of Congress Catalog Card No. 81-84001

© 1982 The STANDARD PUBLISHING Company, Cincinnati, Ohio.
A Division of STANDEX INTERNATIONAL Corporation. Printed in U.S.A.

CONTENTS

INTRODUCTION

Learning centers are an excellent way to provide individualized instruction that motivates the child to seek out information vital to his or her own interests and needs. The child becomes responsible for his/her own learning by setting up, carrying out, and evaluating goals.

Many churches have small classrooms which must be shared with other classes throughout the week. This makes it impossible to leave a large learning center up for any length of time. The centers in this book were kept small and simple to allow for easy storage and quick assembly, yet still provide supplementary and enrichment activities for Bible classes.

A good learning center should incorporate the following characteristics:

- provide individualized instruction by including supplementary, enrichment, or reinforcement material which can be utilized by the child with a minimum of teacher involvement.
- motivate the child to work on exciting, well-planned, and enjoyable activities.
- provide creative and challenging experiences that contribute to the mastering of a multitude of skills and concepts suited to the maturity of the child.
- provide clear, precise visual instructions that tell when and how to use the center. (Auditory reinforcement of instructions should be provided for children who do not read or internalize instructions very well. This can be easily accomplished by taping the written instructions. Encourage the child to try to read the written instructions along with the tape.)
- provide a method of self-checking or group evaluation. The child should be aware of what he/she is expected to learn from the activity.
- provide a choice of manipulative activities as well as written activities for the children.

You can develop your own activities if you follow a few simple rules:

- choose a topic, subject, or skill you wish to include in your basic teaching to reinforce or supplement.
- provide activities that include ways for the child to research specific information, experiment, listen for information or reactions from others, observe or receive information from a human resource such as the minister.
- provide a way for the child to use the information. (Examples: filling out work sheets, working puzzles, playing games, writing stories, matching activities, manipulating devices, and art work.)

As the teacher, you should find and have available as many references as possible about the subject being taught. (Examples: filmstrips, Bible references, Bible dictionary, Bible encyclopedia, concordance, *Webster's Dictionary*, books relating to the subject that are on the children's level, records, pictures, old quarterlies, maps, etc.)

You will also have to collect and organize any material the child might need in order to draw, write, or make a project. The following supplies are only a few of the many possibilities you might include: chalk, crayons, markers, pencils, scissors, glue, stapler, yarn, rulers, old quarterlies for pictures, paper, construction paper, string, watercolors, and clay.

When introducing the center to the entire group be sure to:

- give clear instructions. Even if you have written and taped instructions for the center, give them orally before it is used.
- encourage the children to help one another. Children learn from their peers.
- allow for the display and sharing of the children's work.
- provide and explain the evaluation procedure.
- provide encouragement where needed.
- make the centers as colorful and exciting as possible.

Many of the learning centers suggested in this book can be used for areas of study other than those identified. They can be organized to meet many needs. It is my hope that you will use them in the way that is most suitable for you and your students.

My prayers are with you as you endeavor to bring God's word to those impressionable minds in your charge each Lord's day.

GENERAL INSTRUCTIONS

1. Use legal size folders.
2. Envelopes, either complete or cut in half, will make adequate pockets for small objects and cards.
3. Larger pockets can be formed by cutting a piece of poster board the length you desire and taping it to the folder with colorful plastic tape.
4. Be sure to glue all the pockets so the open end faces the top of the folder when it is shut. This will keep the cards from falling out when the folder is stored.
5. Game boards and some cards can be used directly from the book, or you can trace the boards onto heavier paper and make the cards in a larger size by hand. If you wish to use them directly from the book, these hints will help you:
   - glue the cards to tagboard to increase their durability.
   - use rubber cement rather than white glue in order to prevent wrinkling.
   - it is easier to glue the entire page down, then cut out the individual cards.
   - laminate the finished folders and cards, or cover them with clear contact paper. (The cards should be laminated before cutting them apart.)
6. Instructional tapes are valuable but optional. A sample instructional tape for WHO AM I? TIC-TAC-TOE follows:

Hi, boys and girls! I know you are going to enjoy playing Tic-Tac-Toe with _____ and _____ today. (Insert the names of the Bible characters you have chosen for this activity.)

Read the instructions for this activity with me. They are written on the outside of the folder. (Pause) You will need your Bibles, the Tic-Tac-Toe game board, fact cards, and the X's and O's that are provided on the inside of the folder. Check to make sure they are inside, then shut the folder and read the rest of the instructions with me. (Pause)

You can play this game with another person, with two teams, or as a matching activity by yourself.

How to play:
1. If two children or two teams are playing, decide who will take (Bible character) and who will take (Bible character). (Bible character) gets the X's and (Bible character) gets the O's to mark their answers on the Tic-Tac-Toe game board. Your job is to learn all you can about these two Bible personalities.
2. Take the fact cards out of the pocket, when you are ready to play, and turn them face down on the table. Mix them up.
3. Take the X's and O's out of the pockets and place them in front of you.
4. If it is your turn, choose a card, read it, and decide if it is a Bible fact about your character. If it is, place the card in any position you wish on the Tic-Tac-Toe board. Then place your X or O marker on top of the fact card.
5. If it is not a fact about your character, place the card face up in front of you. In this case, you do not get to place an X or an O on the game board.
6. When it is not your turn, look up the Scripture provided on your opponent's

fact card and check to see if the correct choice was made. If the answer is not correct, *you* may place the card (if it is your own character) on the game board. (Be sure to place a marker over it.) If your opponent's answer was incorrect, and it was his/her own character, he/she loses a turn. Place the card face up in front of your opponent and no one places a marker on the game board.

7. The next player may use the card lying face up in front of the other player, or may draw from the mixed-up cards on the table.

8. After the player chooses a card, it is placed either on the game board or face up in front of him/her while the player's opponent checks the answer.

9. The first player with three markers in a row, related to his/her character, wins the game.

10. If you are the only person using this activity, match the fact cards with a Bible character by laying the cards in a line under the character's name listed at the top of the folder. Check your answers by looking them up in the Bible. This will also help you increase your Bible skills.

Have a good time and remember, "Let us do good unto all men" (Galatians 6:10).

MOSES BLACKOUT

For two children or two teams

Subject: Moses

Bible learning objective: Increasing Bible skills by learning about the life of Moses.

Educational objectives: Searching for information and committing it to memory.

Evaluation procedure: Each child must look up the Scripture in order to check his/her opponent's answer before any points are given.

Materials needed:

   folder, colored poster board, Bibles, felt-tipped marker, glue. (Refer to the general instructions and the diagrams before you begin each folder.)

Directions:

1. Open the folder and transfer the game board as shown. Color the pictures.
2. Draw twenty-four rectangles, one and a half inches by one inch on the poster board, cut them out, and use for covers.
3. Make one pocket to hold the covers. (See inside of folder diagram.)
4. Prepare the outside of the folder as shown in that diagram.

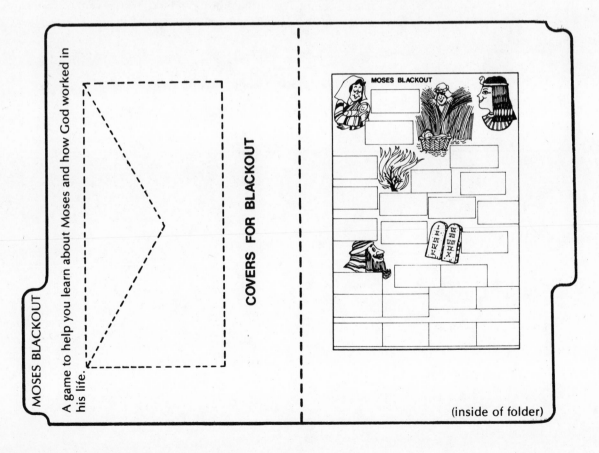

MOSES BLACKOUT

A game to help you learn about Moses and how God worked in his life.

COVERS FOR BLACKOUT

MOSES BLACKOUT

(inside of folder)

Extension:

You can use this basic game board for other subjects:

1. Trace the rectangles on another folder.
2. Find pictures of the subject you wish to study.
3. Glue them in the empty spaces.
4. Type questions about your subject on the rectangles and prepare the folder as you did for this game.
5. Choose an appropriate name such as David Blackout, Bible Blackout, etc.

MOSES BLACKOUT

Who can play:	two players or two teams
You will need:	game board, cover cards, Bibles
How to play:	1. Open the envelope and place the cover cards over the questions on the game board. 2. Decide who will play first. 3. The first player lifts the cover of a question and reads it. 4. If the player can answer the question he/she keeps the cover. 5. As the first player lifts the cover, the second player looks up the Scripture and checks the answer given by the first player. 6. If the player cannot answer the question, he/she replaces the cover. 7. The player or team with the most covers at the end of the game wins. *Whatsoever thy hand findeth to do, do it with thy might.* (Ecclesiastes 9:10) (outside of folder)

Game board

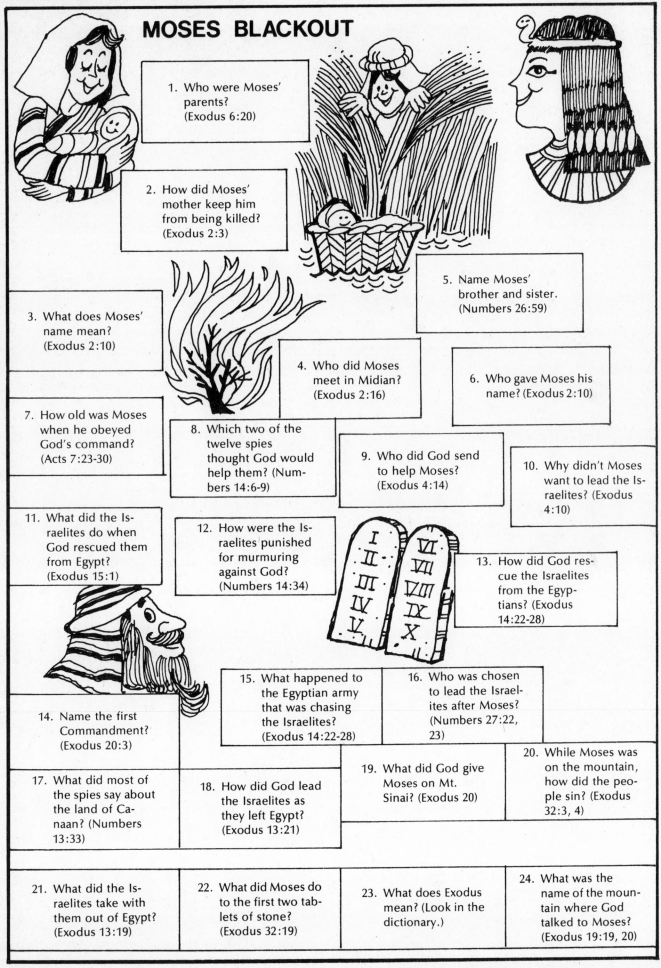

MOSES BLACKOUT

1. Who were Moses' parents? (Exodus 6:20)

2. How did Moses' mother keep him from being killed? (Exodus 2:3)

5. Name Moses' brother and sister. (Numbers 26:59)

3. What does Moses' name mean? (Exodus 2:10)

4. Who did Moses meet in Midian? (Exodus 2:16)

6. Who gave Moses his name? (Exodus 2:10)

7. How old was Moses when he obeyed God's command? (Acts 7:23-30)

8. Which two of the twelve spies thought God would help them? (Numbers 14:6-9)

9. Who did God send to help Moses? (Exodus 4:14)

10. Why didn't Moses want to lead the Israelites? (Exodus 4:10)

11. What did the Israelites do when God rescued them from Egypt? (Exodus 15:1)

12. How were the Israelites punished for murmuring against God? (Numbers 14:34)

13. How did God rescue the Israelites from the Egyptians? (Exodus 14:22-28)

14. Name the first Commandment? (Exodus 20:3)

15. What happened to the Egyptian army that was chasing the Israelites? (Exodus 14:22-28)

16. Who was chosen to lead the Israelites after Moses? (Numbers 27:22, 23)

17. What did most of the spies say about the land of Canaan? (Numbers 13:33)

18. How did God lead the Israelites as they left Egypt? (Exodus 13:21)

19. What did God give Moses on Mt. Sinai? (Exodus 20)

20. While Moses was on the mountain, how did the people sin? (Exodus 32:3, 4)

21. What did the Israelites take with them out of Egypt? (Exodus 13:19)

22. What did Moses do to the first two tablets of stone? (Exodus 32:19)

23. What does Exodus mean? (Look in the dictionary.)

24. What was the name of the mountain where God talked to Moses? (Exodus 19:19, 20)

11

TO THE PROMISED LAND

For two children

Subject: Exodus of the children of Israel from Egypt and their travels to the promised land

Bible learning objectives: Becoming familiar with a Bible map showing the travels of the children of Israel, and learning Bible facts about Moses and the miracles God performed during the journey.

Educational objective: Learning how to use a map to trace specific historical events.

Evaluation procedure: Each child must look up the Scripture in order to check his or her opponent's answer before a move is made on the game board.

Materials needed:
folder, tagboard, poster board, plastic tape, question cards, sponge, two buttons or markers from a discarded game

---

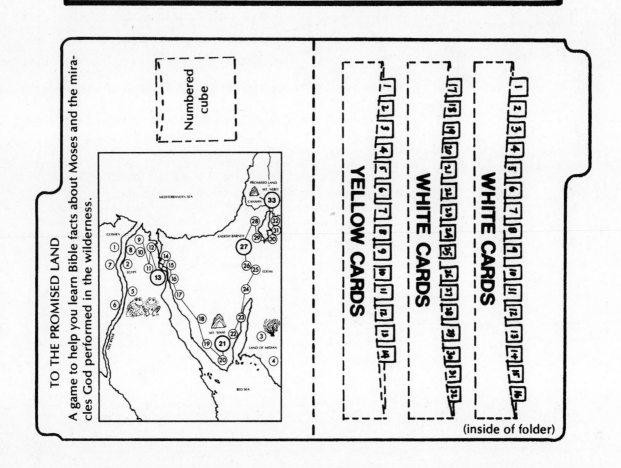

(inside of folder)

Directions:

1. Open the folder and transfer the game board to one side. Color the map to make it more interesting.
2. Make a pocket chart on the other side of the folder: Cut three strips of tagboard, twelve inches by one and one half inches. Tape the strips across the folder with plastic tape. (See diagram.)
3. Make thirty-two cards, two inches by one and one half inches from white poster board, and fourteen cards the same size from yellow poster board. Glue the printed cards to the poster board. (If you want cards with larger print for the children to read, you can easily make your own.)
4. Cut a block from a sponge one inch by one inch. Use a fine line felt-tipped marker to write the numbers one through six on the sides. This numbered cube will fold up in the folder without being bulky. An added bonus is that it won't make any noise when thrown on the table.
5. Place the white cards in the pockets of the chart in numerical order and the yellow cards last.
6. Prepare the outside of the folder as shown in the diagram.

TO THE PROMISED LAND

Who can play:	two players
You will need:	game board, pocket chart, question cards, two markers, one numbered cube
How to play:	1. Decide who will go first. 2. The first player throws the numbered cube and moves the number of spaces shown. 3. If you can answer the question matching the number landed on, you can stay. 4. If you can't answer the question, you must go back where you were. 5. Each player must check the answers of the other players. If he or she gives the wrong answer, the player who looked up the Scripture may move one place without answering another question. 6. If someone is already on a number, the player landing there, too, must answer a gold question. Follow the directions on the card if you answer correctly. If you answer incorrectly, go back to where you were. 7. The first player to the promised land is the winner. *He careth for you.* (1 Peter 5:7) (outside of folder)

1. Who were Moses' parents? (Exodus 6:20)	2. How did Moses' mother protect him from the king? (Exodus 2:3)	3. Who did Moses meet in Midian? (Exodus 2:16)	4. In what unusual way did God call Moses to do a special job? (Exodus 3:2)
5. Why did the Hebrews want to leave Egypt? (Exodus 3:7-9)	6. What did God want Moses to do? (Exodus 3:10)	7. What does Exodus mean? (See dictionary)	8. Name two of the ten disasters that came upon Egypt. (Exodus 7—11)
9. How did God lead the Hebrews as they left Egypt? (Exodus 13:21)	10. What was the name of Moses' sister? (Numbers 26:59)	11. Why didn't Moses want to lead the Hebrews? (Exodus 4:10)	12. Who did God send to help Moses? (Exodus 4:14)
13. What miracle did God perform at the Red Sea? (Exodus 14:22-28)	14. What happened to the Egyptian army that was chasing the Hebrews? (Exodus 14:28)	15. What did the Hebrews do when God rescued them from the Egyptians? (Exodus 15:1)	16. What did the Hebrews take with them out of the land of Egypt? (Exodus 13:19)
17. How did God feed the people in the wilderness? (Exodus 16:35)	18. In what part of the Bible will you find Exodus and Numbers?	19. What was the name of Moses' brother? (Numbers 26:59)	20. What was the name of the mountain where God talked to Moses? (Exodus 19:19, 20)
21. What did God give Moses on Mt. Sinai? (Exodus 20)	22. What were the people doing while Moses was with God? (Exodus 32:1-6)	23. Name the first Commandment. (Exodus 20:3)	24. What did God tell Moses to build? (Exodus 40:2)
25. What did Moses do to the first tablets of stone? (Exodus 32:19)	26. Which two of the twelve spies thought God would help Israel take the land? (Numbers 14:6-8)	27. Who was to be the chief priest of the tabernacle? (Exodus 28:1)	28. How were the Hebrews punished for murmuring against Moses and God? (Numbers 14:34)
29. Who was chosen to lead the people after Moses died? (Numbers 27:22, 23)	30. How old was Moses when he died? (Deuteronomy 34:7)	31. What did most of the spies say about the land of Canaan? (Numbers 13:33)	32. What did the Hebrews promise God and Moses? (Exodus 24:7)

		1. Name the river where baby Moses was found. (Exodus 1:22, *Living Bible*) MOVE AHEAD ONE	2. What job did Moses do for Jethro? (Exodus 3:1) GO AHEAD TWO
3. Did Moses cross into Canaan? (Deuteronomy 31:2) GO AHEAD TWO	4. Where did Moses go to see Canaan? (Deuteronomy 32:49) GO AHEAD TWO	5. Why did Moses leave Egypt? (Exodus 2:11-15) MOVE AHEAD TWO	6. "In all thy ways acknowledge him, and he shall ___." (Proverbs 3:6) GO AHEAD TWO
7. Moses' mother placed him in a basket ____. (Exodus 2:3) MOVE AHEAD TWO	8. Who gave Moses his name? (Exodus 2:10) MOVE AHEAD THREE	9. Name Moses' father-in-law. (Exodus 3:1) MOVE AHEAD ONE	10. "Thou shalt do that which is right and good ____." (Deuteronomy 6:18) MOVE AHEAD TWO
11. What does Moses' name mean? (Exodus 2:10) MOVE AHEAD TWO	12. Who watched over Moses at the river? (Exodus 2:4) MOVE AHEAD THREE	13. "We ought to obey God rather ____." (Acts 5:29) MOVE AHEAD TWO	14. "All that the Lord hath said ____." (Exodus 24:7) GO AHEAD ONE

MEDITERRANEAN SEA

PROMISED LAND

MT. NEBO

CANAAN

33

28

32

KADESH BARNEA

31

GOSHEN

9

29

30

1

12

27

8

10

14

26

25

EDOM

7

2

15

11

EGYPT

13

24

16

5

17

23

6

3

18

MT. SINAI

22

19

21

LAND OF MIDIAN

NILE RIVER

20

4

RED SEA

BIBLE FOOTBALL

For two or more children
Subject: Joseph
Bible learning objective: Learning about Joseph's life.
Educational objectives: Seeking information and committing it to memory.
Evaluation procedure: The children check their opponents' answers by looking up the Scriptures before any player receives yardage or points.

Materials needed:
folder, patterns, questions, sponge, felt-tipped marker, two playing pieces or buttons, pencil, paper, Bible

---

Directions:
1. Open the folder and position the pockets as shown in the diagram.
2. Prepare the game board and insert it inside the folder. (See #6)
3. Prepare the outside of the folder as shown in the diagram.

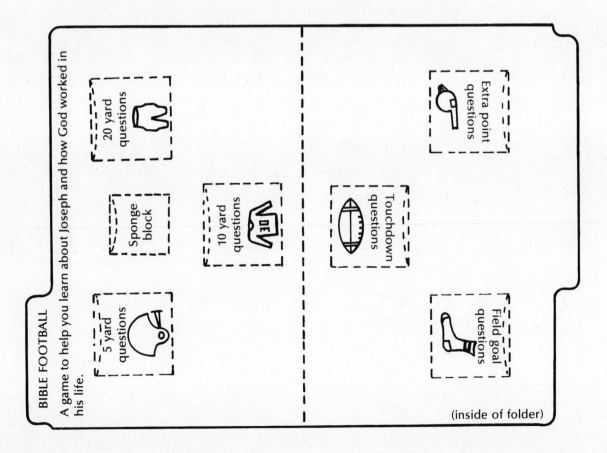

BIBLE FOOTBALL
A game to help you learn about Joseph and how God worked in his life.

20 yard questions

Sponge block

10 yard questions

5 yard questions

Extra point questions

Touchdown questions

Field goal questions

(inside of folder)

4. Make the question cards. (Questions are provided.)
5. Cut a one-inch block from the sponge. On this block mark two opposite sides with a 5, two opposite sides with a 10, and two opposite sides with a 20.
6. The game board is made from two sheets of construction paper. Make two sheets from the pattern and lap the right 50 yard line over the left 50 yard line. Tape on both sides. Insert the folded game board inside the folder.

Extension:

This game can be extended to many other subjects by changing the questions. Be sure to make your touchdown, field goal, and bonus point questions more difficult than your yardage questions. Preparing a different folder for each subject facilitates storage and filing.

BIBLE FOOTBALL

Who can play:	two players or two teams
You will need:	game board, question cards, numbered block, pencil, score sheet
How to play:	1. Each team chooses a goal and places its marker facing the other team on the 50 yard line. (Throw the sponge block. High number goes first.) 2. Throw the block again. Choose a question from the pocket that has the same number you threw. Advance five yards for each question on a helmet, ten yards for each question on a jersey, and twenty yards for each question on the pants. 3. When a team advances to the five yard line, they may draw a question from the touchdown pocket. If answered correctly, you score six points. 4. You can answer a field-goal question from the 15 yard line to score three points if you see you aren't going to make it to the 5 yard line. 5. After a touchdown is scored, a team can draw from the bonus pocket to score an extra point. 6. If the offensive team cannot answer a question, the defensive team gets a chance. If the defensive team *can* answer the question, the offensive team must go back the number of yards indicated on the question. 7. The defensive team may look up the answers in the Bible to check the offensive team's answers and be ready to answer the question should the offensive team fail to do so. 8. When points are scored, the teams return to the 50 yard line. The offensive team then becomes the defensive team and vice versa. 9. Each team may draw only four questions each turn in their effort to score a touchdown. If they are unable to make a touchdown in four tries, they must return to the 50 yard line where the opposing team begins their turn. 10. The winner is the team with the most points at the end of play. *The Lord hath done great things for us; whereof we are glad.* (Psalm 126:3) (outside of folder)

Five-Yard Questions:

1. How many sons did Jacob have? (Genesis 35:22)
2. What did Jacob give to Joseph? (Genesis 37:3)
3. Why did the brothers hate Joseph? (Genesis 37:4)
4. Why did Joseph's brothers go to Shechem? (Genesis 37:12)
5. Why did Jacob send Joseph to Shechem? (Genesis 37:14)
6. What did the brothers plot to do when they saw Joseph coming? (Genesis 37:18)
7. Who came along while the brothers were eating lunch? (Genesis 37:25)
8. Who thought of another plan to get rid of Joseph when they saw the Ishmaelites? (Genesis 37:26)
9. What did the brothers tell Jacob? (Genesis 37:32)
10. Who were the two men in prison with Joseph? (Genesis 40:2)
11. What did Joseph ask the chief butler to do when he got out of prison? (Genesis 40:14, 15)
12. Did the chief butler do as Joseph asked? (Genesis 40:23)
13. What did Joseph order his servant to do when the brothers were ready to leave Egypt the second time? (Genesis 44:1-6)
14. What did Jacob do when he learned there was grain in Egypt? (Genesis 42:2)
15. Why didn't Benjamin go with his older brothers when they went to Egypt to buy grain? (Genesis 42:4)
16. What did Joseph accuse the brothers of doing when he recognized them? (Genesis 42:9)

Ten-Yard Questions:

1. What was the first dream Joseph had? (Genesis 37:7)
2. What was the second dream Joseph had? (Genesis 37:9)
3. What was the plan Reuben suggested to his brothers? (Genesis 37:22)
4. How much money did the brothers get from the Midianite traders? (Genesis 37:28)
5. What did the brothers do with Joseph's coat? (Genesis 37:31)
6. Where did the traders take Joseph? (Genesis 37:36)
7. Who lied about Joseph to Potiphar? (Genesis 39:19)
8. What was the dream of the chief butler? (Genesis 40:9, 10)
9. What was the dream of the chief baker? (Genesis 40:16-18)
10. Describe the first dream Pharaoh had. (Genesis 41:1-4)
11. Describe Pharaoh's second dream. (Genesis 41:5-7)
12. What did Joseph tell Pharaoh about the meaning of the dreams? (Genesis 41:26-32)
13. What plan did Joseph propose to Pharaoh? (Genesis 41:33-36)
14. What happened that was the fulfillment of Joseph's boyhood dreams? (Genesis 42:6-9)
15. What were Joseph's orders to the servants concerning the payment the brothers had made for the grain? (Genesis 42:25)
16. What did Joseph do when he saw that the brothers had returned? (Genesis 43:16)
17. Where did Pharaoh give Joseph's family permission to settle down in the land of Egypt? (Genesis 47:6)

Twenty-Yard Questions:

1. Where did Jacob settle down to live and raise his family? (Genesis 37:1)
2. What did Jacob say about the second dream of Joseph? (Genesis 37:10)
3. Where had the brothers gone from Shechem? (Genesis 37:17)
4. Who thought of an alternative plan that kept the brothers from killing Joseph? (Genesis 37:21)
5. Who bought Joseph from the slave traders? (Genesis 37:36)
6. What did the jailer do with Joseph after he got to know him? (Genesis 39:22)
7. Who did the brothers have to talk to in order to buy grain? (Genesis 42:6)
8. What did Joseph tell the brothers they must do to prove that they weren't spies? (Genesis 42:14-16)
9. Why did the brothers think this trouble had come to them? (Genesis 42:21)
10. What did Jacob tell the brothers to do when he realized they had to return to Egypt a second time? (Genesis 43:11-14)
11. What happened when Joseph saw Benjamin? (Genesis 43:30)
12. What did the brothers promise the servant they would do if the cup were found in their grain sacks? (Genesis 44:9)
13. What was Jacob's other name? (Genesis 35:10)

Field-Goal Questions:

1. What was Judah's plan that the brothers decided to follow in order to get rid of Joseph? (Genesis 37:27)
2. What was the meaning of the chief butler's dream? (Genesis 40:12, 13)
3. What was the meaning of the chief baker's dream? (Genesis 40:18, 19)
4. What did Pharaoh do when he heard the chief butler's story? (Genesis 41:14)
5. How old was Joseph when he was sold into slavery? (Genesis 37:2)
6. Who gave Joseph the interpretation of the dreams? (Genesis 40:8)
7. What did the chief butler tell Pharaoh when no one was found to interpret Pharaoh's dream? (Genesis 41:10-13)
8. Who did Pharaoh appoint to carry out Joseph's plan? (Genesis 41:40)
9. What did Reuben promise his father about Benjamin? (Genesis 42:37)
10. Why did Joseph think he had been sent to Egypt? (Genesis 45:5-8)

Touchdown Questions:

1. "Every good gift and every perfect _____ is from _____ , and cometh down from the Father" (James 1:17).
2. "All things were _____ by him; and without him was not any thing _____ that was _____" (John 1:3).
3. "_____ shall supply all your _____" (Philippians 4:19).
4. "Blessed are they that _____ the _____ of _____ , and keep it" (Luke 11:28).
5. "God is our refuge and strength, a very present _____ in _____" (Psalm 46:1).
6. "Thou, Lord, art _____ , and ready to _____" (Psalm 86:5).
7. "The _____ is nigh unto all them that _____ upon him"

(Psalm 145:18).

8. "The Lord is the _____ of my life; of whom shall I be _____" (Psalm 27:1)?

9. "Thou art near, O _____ ; and all thy _____ are truth . . ." (Psalm 119:151).

10. "I will instruct thee and _____ thee in the way which thou _____ _____" (Psalm 32:8).

11. "Behold, _____ is mine _____" (Psalm 54:4).

12. "(God) _____ _____ , and sent his _____" (1 John 4:10).

13. "Be _____ and of good courage; be not _____ , neither be thou dismayed: for the _____ thy God is with thee withersoever thou goest" (Joshua 1:9).

14. "Blessed be the _____ , . . . there hath not failed one _____ of all his good _____" (1 Kings 8:56).

Extra-Point Questions:

1. In which book of the Bible will you find the story of Joseph?
2. What is the name of the most important river in Egypt? (Genesis 41:1, *Living Bible*)
3. Why did Pharaoh hold a feast three days after Joseph interpreted the dreams of the chief baker and the chief butler? (Genesis 40:20)
4. Why did both of Pharaoh's dreams mean the same thing? (Genesis 41:32)
5. What did Pharaoh give Joseph as a sign of his authority? (Genesis 41:42)
6. How old was Joseph when he was placed in charge of all the land of Egypt? (Genesis 41:46)
7. What did Joseph name his two sons? (Genesis 41:50-52)
8. In what land was Jacob living when he sent his sons to buy food in Egypt? (Genesis 42:13)
9. Why did the brothers think they were being taken to Joseph's home when they returned to Egypt the second time? (Genesis 43:18)
10. Why didn't Joseph eat with his brothers? (Genesis 43:32)

Patterns for Bible Football Questions

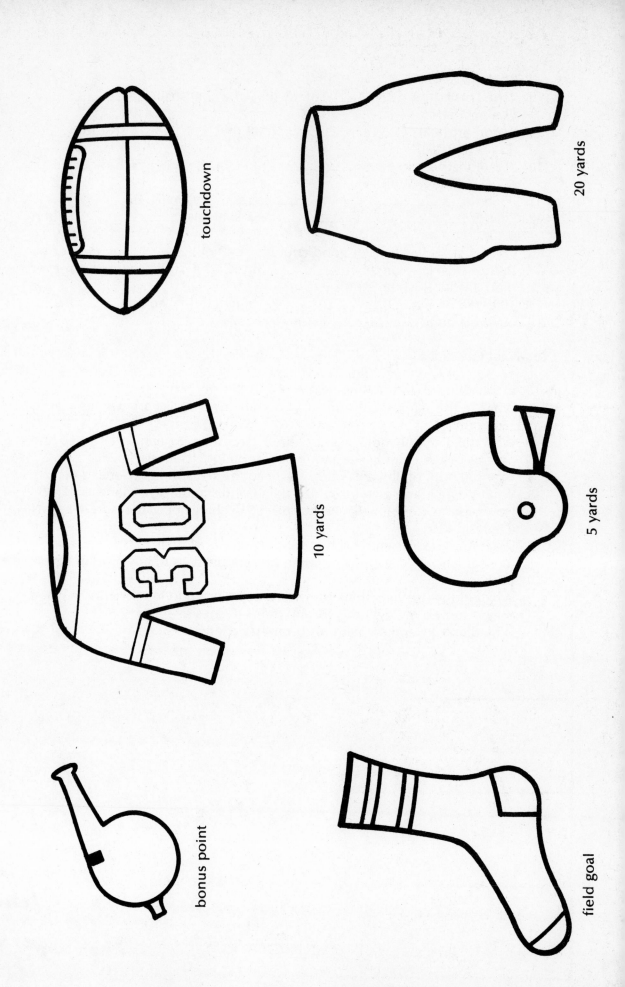

touchdown

20 yards

10 yards

5 yards

bonus point

field goal

Game board

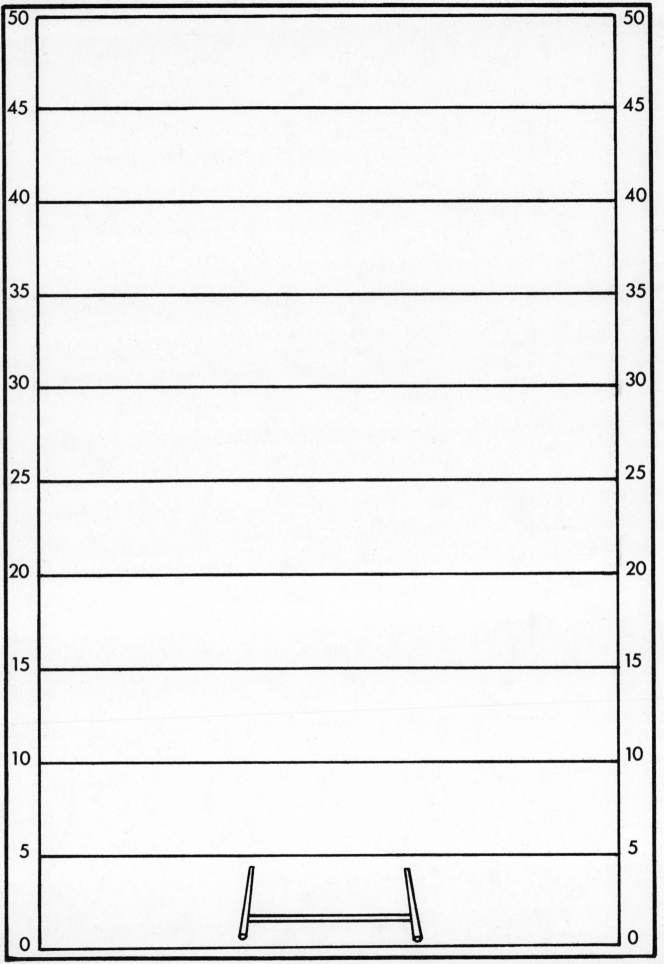

PENNY ROLL

For two players or two teams

Subject: Joseph

Bible learning objectives: Learning facts about the life of Joseph and acquiring Bible skills.

Educational objectives: Searching for information and committing it to memory.

Evaluation procedure: Each player checks the answer of his opponent by looking up the Scripture provided, before points are given.

Materials needed:

folder, two pennies, red, yellow, blue, and green poster board, score paper, pencil, glue

---

Directions:

1. Open the folder and transfer the game board. Color five of the squares red, five blue, five yellow, and five green. (Space the colors so none are grouped together.) Color one circle red and the other circle blue.

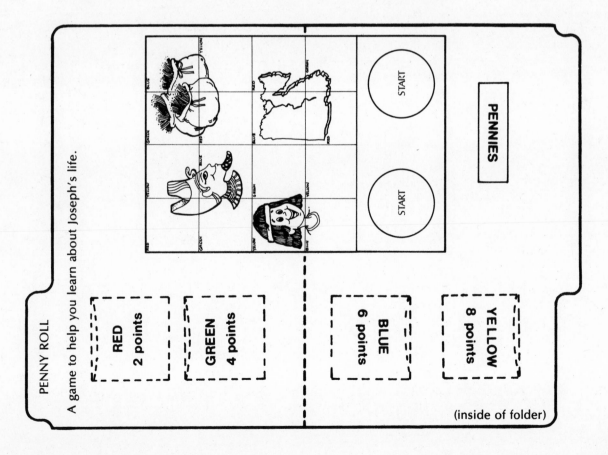

PENNY ROLL

A game to help you learn about Joseph's life.

START

START

PENNIES

RED 2 points

GREEN 4 points

BLUE 6 points

YELLOW 8 points

(inside of folder)

2. Tear out question pages, glue to colored cards, and cut them apart.
3. There are fourteen, two by two inch, red poster board question cards, seventeen green cards, sixteen blue, and thirteen yellow. (See directions for making cards in the general instructions at the beginning of this book.)
4. Prepare the outside of the folder as shown.

PENNY ROLL	
Who can play:	two players or two teams
You will need:	two pennies, question cards, game board, score sheet and pencil
How to play:	1. Decide who will play first and which circle each will use. 2. Place your penny on its edge in your circle. 3. Roll the penny down the game board. 4. Your team receives one half of the question points for landing on a square and one half of the points when you answer the question correctly. 5. The opposing team looks up the answer while the scoring team gives the answer. If the answer isn't correct, the opposing team gets one half of the points for that question. 6. There is a one point penalty if your penny rolls off the table. 7. The winner is the team with the most points. *Whatsoever thy hand findeth to do, do it with thy might.* (Ecclesiastes 9:10) (outside of folder)

1. Why did Jacob love Joseph more than the other brothers? (Genesis 37:3) 2 points

2. What was one of the dreams Joseph had about his brothers? (Genesis 37:7-9) 2 points

3. What did Jacob think about Joseph when he had the dreams? (Genesis 37:10, 11) 2 points

4. How old was Joseph when he helped his brothers take care of the sheep? (Genesis 37:2) 2 points

5. Name one reason Joseph's brothers disliked him. (Genesis 37:2, 3, 11) 2 points

6. What was the brothers' first plan when they saw Joseph? (Genesis 37:19, 20) 2 points

7. What did Joseph do when he was helping his brothers with the sheep that made them hate him even more? (Genesis 37:2) 2 points

8. Why did Jacob send Joseph away from home? (Genesis 37:13, 14) 2 points

9. What did the brothers think about Joseph's dream? (Genesis 37:8) 2 points

10. Where did Joseph find his brothers? (Genesis 37:17) 2 points

11. What did the brothers tell Jacob? (Genesis 37:32) 2 points

12. How did God bless Potiphar while Joseph was his slave? (Genesis 39:5) 4 points

13. What two men did Joseph meet in prison? (Genesis 40:1-3) 4 points

14. Who suggested they throw Joseph into a pit? (Genesis 37:22) 2 points

15. To what land was Joseph taken? (Genesis 37:28) 4 points

16. Who tried to trick Joseph? (Genesis 39:7) 4 points

17. Tell about the dream of the chief baker. (Genesis 40:16, 17) 4 points

18. Who suggested they sell Joseph to the Ishmaelites? (Genesis 37:26, 27) 2 points

19. What happened to Joseph when he arrived in the land of Egypt? (Genesis 37:36) 4 points

20. What did Potiphar do to Joseph when he heard the lie from his wife? (Genesis 39:20) 4 points

21. Tell about the dream of the chief butler. (Genesis 40:9-11) 4 points

22. What did the brothers do with Joseph's coat? (Genesis 37:31) 2 points

23. Who bought Joseph from the Ishmaelites? (Genesis 39:1) 4 points

24. What did the keeper of the prison do with Joseph? (Genesis 39:22, 23) 4 points

25. What did the dream of the chief butler mean? (Genesis 40:12, 13) 4 points

26. What did the dream of the chief baker mean? (Genesis 40:18, 19) 4 points

27. Why did Pharaoh send for Joseph? (Genesis 41:15) 4 points

28. Why did Pharaoh set Joseph up as the governor of Egypt? (Genesis 41:39) 6 points

29. What was Joseph's job during the seven good years? (Genesis 41:48) 6 points

30. What did Joseph ask the chief butler to do when he had been restored to his job? (Genesis 40:14) 4 points

31. Who did Joseph say could interpret the dream? (Genesis 41:16)
4 points

32. How old was Joseph when he was made the governor of Egypt? (Genesis 41:46)
6 points

33. What happened when the seven good years Joseph predicted came to an end? (Genesis 41:53, 54)
6 points

34. Did the chief butler remember his promise? (Genesis 40:23)
4 points

35. What did Pharaoh's dream mean? (Genesis 41:26-31)
6 points

36. Name Joseph's two sons. (Genesis 41:51, 52)
6 points

37. What did Jacob want to do when he heard there was grain in Egypt? (Genesis 42:2)
6 points

38. Tell about one of the dreams of Pharaoh. (Genesis 41:2-7)
4 points

39. What was Joseph's suggestion to Pharaoh after he had interpreted the dream? (Genesis 41:34-36)
6 points

40. Why wouldn't Jacob allow Benjamin to go to Egypt with his brothers? (Genesis 42:4)
6 points

41. Who did Jacob send to Egypt to buy grain? (Genesis 42:3)
6 points

42. What did Joseph say to his brothers when he recognized them? (Genesis 42:8, 9)
6 points

43. How did Jacob reply when his sons had told him what had happened in Egypt? (Genesis 42:38)
6 points

44. What did the brothers promise to do if the cup were found with one of them? (Genesis 44:9)
8 points

45. What did Joseph tell the brothers they must do to prove they weren't spies? (Genesis 42:9)
6 points

46. What did Jacob's sons take back with them when they returned to Egypt? (Genesis 43:11-13)
6 points

47. What did the brothers do when they found the cup in Benjamin's sack? (Genesis 44:13)
8 points

48. How did Joseph's boyhood dreams come true? (Genesis 42:6-9)
8 points

49. Which of the brothers did Joseph select to stay in Egypt while the others went back? (Genesis 42:24)
6 points

50. How did Joseph treat his brothers the second time they came with Benjamin? (Genesis 43:31-34)
8 points

51. What did Joseph do when he realized that his brothers had changed? (Genesis 45:1, 2)
8 points

52. "Behold, _____ is mine _____." (Psalm 54:4)
8 points

53. What did the brothers find in their sacks of grain when they returned? (Genesis 42:28)
6 points

54. What did Joseph order his steward to do when the brothers were ready to go back to Canaan? (Genesis 44:1, 2)
8 points

55. Which brother begged Joseph for Benjamin's life? (Genesis 44:18)
8 points

56. "Lead _____ in thy _____, and _____ me." (Psalm 25:5)
8 points

57. "For thou, _____, art _____, and _____, ready to _____." (Psalm 86:5)
8 points

58. "God is our _____, and strength, a very present help in _____." (Psalm 46:1)
8 points

59. "The Lord thy God, . . . doth go with thee in all _____." (Deuteronomy 31:6)
8 points

60. "I am with thee, and will _____ thee in all _____." (Genesis 28:15)
8 points

Game board

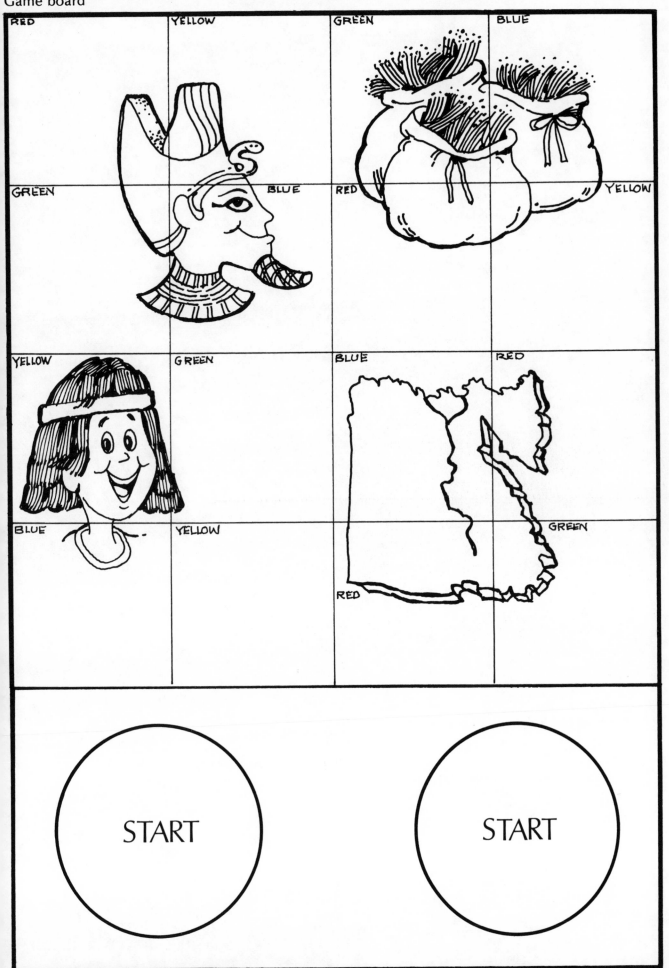

JOSEPH WORD FIND

Any number of children
Subject: Joseph
Bible learning objective: Learning Bible facts about Joseph.
Educational objective: Seeking answers from a specific source.
Evaluation procedure: Check sheet.

Materials needed:
  folder, poster board, scissors, crayons or felt-tipped markers, Joseph's coat pattern, work sheet, Bible, pencil

---

Directions:
1. Duplicate the coats and word find.
2. Duplicate the work sheets. Fill out one with a red marker to be used as an answer sheet.
3. Prepare the inside and outside of the folder as shown in the diagrams.

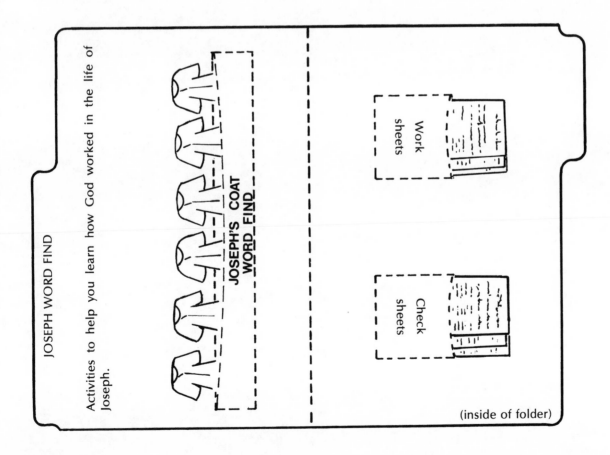

JOSEPH WORD FIND

Activities to help you learn how God worked in the life of Joseph.

JOSEPH'S COAT WORD FIND

Work sheets

Check sheets

(inside of folder)

JOSEPH WORD FIND

Who can use:	anyone
You will need:	work sheet, check sheet, Joseph's Coat Word Find, pencils, Bibles, crayons or felt-tipped markers
How to use:	1. Fill in the work sheet. Use your Bible to find the answers. 2. Use the answer sheet to check your answers. 3. The answers you find on the work sheet will be the words to look for in the Joseph's Coat Word Find. 4. Color Joseph's coat. *Teach me to do thy will; for thou art my God.* (Psalm 143:10) (outside of folder)

Use the Bible to find the answers to these questions about Joseph. Check your answers with the answer sheet, then use the answers from this work sheet to find and circle words on the Joseph's Coat Word Find.

1. Isaac was Jacob's _____. (Genesis 27:22)

2. The dreams of the Pharaoh foretold a _____ in the land. (Genesis 41:27)

3. Joseph's brothers planned to _____ him. (Genesis 37:18)

4. Joseph had eleven _____. (Genesis 35:22)

5. The brothers went to Egypt to buy _____. (Genesis 42:3)

6. Reuben wanted the brothers to put Joseph in the _____. (Genesis 37:22)

7. Jacob gave Joseph a _____ of many colors. (Genesis 37:3)

8. The butler told Pharaoh that Joseph could interpret his strange _____. (Genesis 41:15)

9. Benjamin found Joseph's _____ in his sack of grain. (Genesis 44:2, 12)

10. _____ told Jacob he would be responsible for Benjamin while the brothers were in Egypt. (Genesis 43:8, 9)

11. Joseph told his brothers who he was and sent them to get his father who was named _____. (Genesis 45:25, 26)

12. _____ thought of the plan to sell Joseph to the Ishmaelites. (Genesis 37:26, 27)

13. Joseph was sold as a slave in the land of _____. (Genesis 37:28)

14. The _____ was angry with the chief baker and the chief butler. (Genesis 40:2)

15. Joseph told Pharaoh that _____ was the one who could interpret dreams. (Genesis 40:8)

16. The chief _____ was hanged as Joseph said. (Genesis 40:22)

17. The chief _____ forgot his promise to Joseph. (Genesis 40:23)

18. Color Joseph's coat the way you imagine it looked after you have found these answers in the word find.

Joseph's Coat Word Find

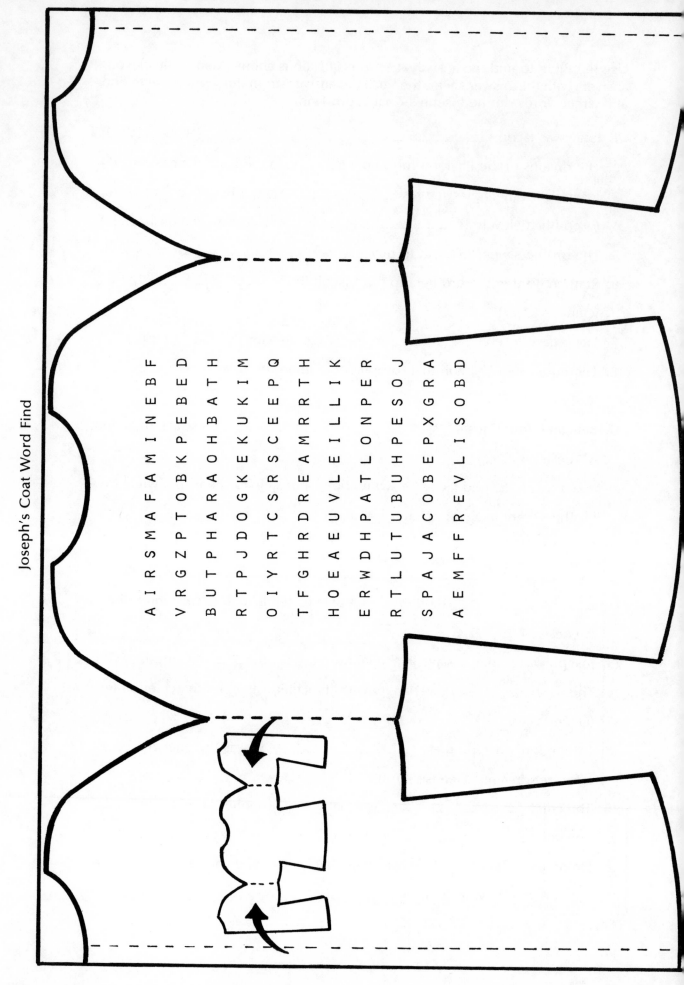

A I R S M A F A M I N E B F
V R G Z P T O B K P E B E D
B U T P H A R A O H B A T H
R T P J D O G K E K U K I M
O I Y R T C S R S C E E P Q
T F G H R D R E A M R R T H
H O E A E U V L E I L L I K
E R W D H P A T L O N P E R
R T L U T U B U H P E S O J
S P A J A C O B E P X G R A
A E M F F R E V L I S O B D

38

PENNY SLIDE

For two or more players or two teams

Subject: David

Bible learning objective: Learning how God worked in the life of David.

Educational objectives: Seeking information and committing it to memory.

Evaluation procedure: Each child is responsible for looking up the answers to the questions before points are given to his/her opponent.

Materials needed:
folder, envelopes, glue, scissors, poster board, score paper, pencil, two pennies

---

Directions:

1. Open the folder and transfer the game board. Color the sections as indicated.
2. Transfer the question cards to two by two inch poster board.
3. Prepare the inside and outside of the folder as shown in the diagrams.

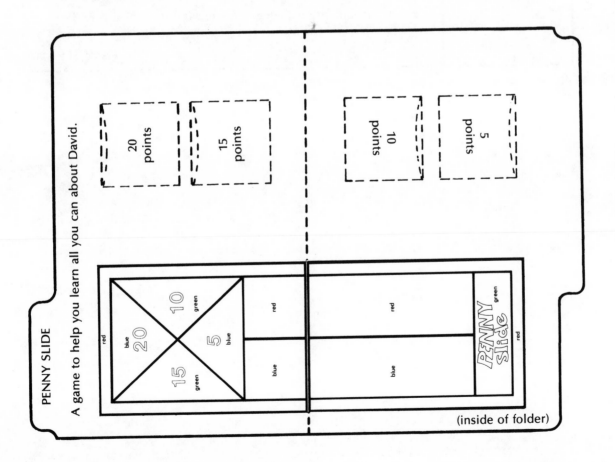

(inside of folder)

Extension:

Make Bible questions for other topics and use this game board pattern. Graduate the difficulty of the questions.

PENNY SLIDE	
Who can play:	two players or two teams
You will need:	pencils, two pennies, game board, Bible questions, Bible, *Living Bible*, score paper
How to play:	1. The first player places his penny in the box marked "penny slide."
	2. Use the eraser of your pencil to push the penny down the red lane.
	3. Choose a question from the pocket marked with the same number as the box where your penny lands.
	4. If you answer the question correctly, you receive that number of points.
	5. On your next turn, you must push your penny down the blue lane.
	6. If it isn't your turn, you must look up the Scripture indicated on your opponent's question to check the answer given by the other team.
	7. If your opponent doesn't answer the question correctly, you receive 10 points.
	8. The winner is the team with the most points at the end of play.
	Hear instruction, and be wise, and refuse it not. (Proverbs 8:33)
	(outside of folder)

Question cards:

1. Who was David's father? (1 Samuel 16:11) 5 points

2. Who were the armies of king Saul fighting? (1 Samuel 17:1) 5 points

3. How did Saul and his men feel when they heard Goliath issue his challenge? (1 Samuel 17:11) 5 points

4. What did Jesse tell David to do? (1 Samuel 17:17) 10 points

5. What prophet anointed David as king of Israel when he was a boy? (1 Samuel 16:13) 5 points

6. How tall was Goliath? (*Living Bible*, 1 Samuel 17:4) 5 points

7. How many sons did Jesse have? (1 Samuel 17:12) 5 points

8. What did David do for the sheep before he went to find his brothers? (1 Samuel 17:20) 10 points

9. Why did Saul need someone to play the harp for him? (1 Samuel 16:16) 5 points

10. What was the name of the Philistine giant? (1 Samuel 17:4) 5 points

11. How many sons of Jesse had followed Saul into battle? (1 Samuel 17:13) 5 points

12. What did Saul promise to the man who killed Goliath? (1 Samuel 17:25) 10 points

13. What did Jesse send along with David to king Saul? (1 Samuel 16:20) 5 points

14. What did Goliath say to the Israelites every day? (1 Samuel 17:8, 9) 5 points

15. Who was the youngest son of Jesse? (1 Samuel 17:14) 5 points

16. What did David say when he heard Goliath shout at the Israelite army? (1 Samuel 17:26) 10 points

17. What did David's brother say to him? (1 Samuel 17:28) 10 points

18. What brave deed did David tell Saul about to prove he wasn't too young to fight the giant? (1 Samuel 17:34) 10 points

19. What did Goliath say he was going to do to David? (1 Samuel 17:43, 44) 15 points

20. What did Jonathan give to David? (1 Samuel 18:4) 15 points

21. What did David tell Saul he would do? (1 Samuel 17:32) 10 points

22. Who did David give glory for saving him from the bear and the lion? (1 Samuel 17:37) 10 points

23. What was David's reply to Goliath? (1 Samuel 17:46, 47) 15 points

24. Why was Saul jealous of David? (1 Samuel 18:7, 8) 15 points

25. How did Saul answer when David offered to kill Goliath? (1 Samuel 17:33) 10 points

26. Who did David count on to save him from the giant? (1 Samuel 17:37) 10 points

27. How did David kill Goliath? (1 Samuel 17:50, 51) 15 points

28. What did Saul try to do that caused David to run away? (1 Samuel 19:10) 15 points

29. What did Saul try to give David before he fought the giant? (1 Samuel 17:38, 39) 15 points

30. What did David take for a weapon to fight Goliath? (1 Samuel 17:40) 15 points

41

36. "Be of good ——, and he shall strengthen your ——, all ye that hope in the Lord." (Psalm 31:24)
20 points

37. Where did David live one time while he was hiding from Saul? (1 Samuel 21:1)
15 points

38. "But know that the Lord hath set apart him that is —— for himself: The Lord will —— when I call unto him." (Psalm 4:3)
20 points

39. "Let the —— of my mouth, and the meditation of my ——, be acceptable in thy sight, O Lord." (Psalm 19:14)
20 points

40. "For the word of the Lord is ——; and all his works are done in ——." (Psalm 33:4)
20 points

35. "I will —— thee, O Lord, my strength." (Psalm 18:1)
20 points

34. "But thou, O Lord, art a shield for me; my glory, and the —— of mine head." (Psalm 3:3)
20 points

33. How did Jonathan warn David about his father's plans? (1 Samuel 20:19-22)
15 points

32. What did David and Jonathan promise to one another? (1 Samuel 20:42)
15 points

31. Who became David's best friend? (1 Samuel 18:1)
15 points

red

blue

20

15
green

10
green

5
blue

blue

red

(Lap the other part of the game board over this flap and glue.)

43

41. What did David do when he could have killed Saul? (1 Samuel 24:4-10)
20 points

42. "My voice shalt thou hear in the morning, O Lord; in the morning will I direct my ——— unto thee, and will look up." (Psalm 5:3)
20 points

43. "He restoreth my soul: he ——— me in the paths of righteousness for his name's sake." (Psalm 23:3)
20 points

44. "God is our ——— and ———, a very present help in ———." (Psalm 46:1)
20 points

45. Tell about another time that David spared the life of king Saul when he could have killed him. (1 Samuel 26:7-12)
20 points

46. "And they that know thy name will put their ——— in thee: for thou, Lord, hast not forsaken them that ——— thee." (Psalm 9:10)
20 points

47. "Shew me thy ways, O Lord; ——— me thy ———." (Psalm 25:4)
20 points

48. "For this God is ——— for ever and ever: he will be our ——— even unto death." (Psalm 48:14)
20 points

blue

red

PENNY Slide

green

red

Game board

45

MYSTERY MESSAGE

For any number of children
Subject: Zaccheus
Bible learning objective: Discovering what Zaccheus learned from Jesus.
Educational objectives: Finding information and committing it to memory.
Evaluation procedure: Group discussion.

> **Materials needed:**
>   one and one-half folders, work sheets, crayons or markers, Bible, pencils

Directions:
1. Prepare the inside, outside, and extra insertion folders as shown in the diagrams.
2. Duplicate the work sheets.

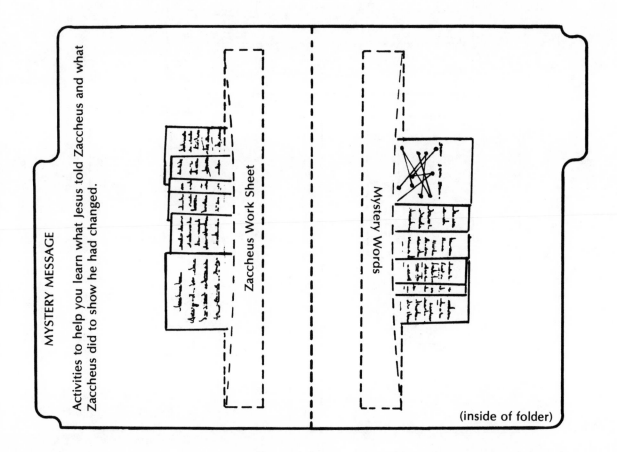

MYSTERY MESSAGE

Activities to help you learn what Jesus told Zaccheus and what Zaccheus did to show he had changed.

Zaccheus Work Sheet

Mystery Words

(inside of folder)

MYSTERY MESSAGE

Who can use:	anyone
You will need:	work sheets, crayons or felt-tipped markers, pencils, Bibles: *Living Bible, Revised Standard, New International, King James* versions
How to use:	1. Answer the questions on the Zaccheus Work Sheet. 2. Choose any of the other activities and follow the directions. *While we were yet sinners, Christ died for us.* (Romans 5:8) (outside of folder)

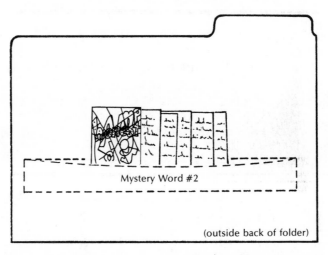

Mystery Word #2

(outside back of folder)

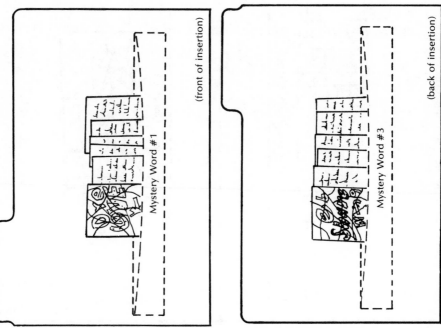

Mystery Word #1

(front of insertion)

Mystery Word #3

(back of insertion)

ZACCHEUS WORK SHEET

1. What city was Jesus visiting when he met Zaccheus? _____

_____ (Luke 19:1)

2. What kind of business was Zaccheus in? _____

(See Luke 19:2 in the *Living Bible, New International,* or *Revised Standard.*)

3. Why couldn't Zaccheus see Jesus? _____ (Luke 19:3)

4. What did Zaccheus do so he could see Jesus? _____ (Luke 19:4)

5. What kind of tree did Zaccheus climb? _____ (Luke 19:4)

6. Where did Jesus want to go? _____ (Luke 19:5)

7. What did Jesus say to Zaccheus? _____ (Luke 19:5)

8. What did the crowd say when Jesus went home with Zaccheus? _____

_____ (Luke 19:7)

9. What did Zaccheus promise to do for those he had overcharged? _____

_____ (Luke 19:8)

10. What did Zaccheus promise Jesus he would do for the poor? _____

_____

_____ (Luke 19:8)

11. What did Jesus say to Zaccheus when he promised to give one half of his

money to the poor? _____ (Luke 19:9)

12. "For the Son of Man is come to _____ and to _____

that which was _____." (Luke 19:10)

Trace each line from letter to letter to name four things Zaccheus learned from Jesus. Write them below.

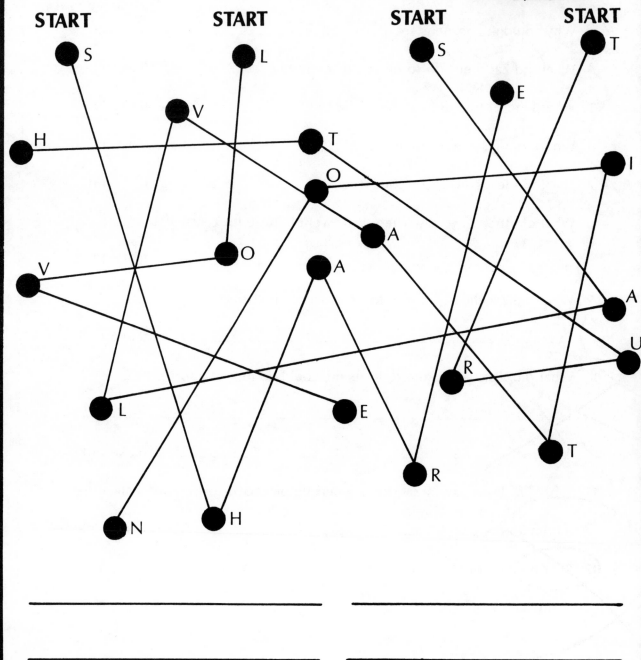

START **START** **START** **START**

S   L   S   T
V   E
H   T   I
O
A   A
V   A
U
L   E   R
R   T
N   H

_____   _____

_____   _____

50

Color all the sections that have an X in them. The secret message is _____.

Mystery Word #1

Color all the sections that have an X in them. The secret message is ——————.

Color all the sections that have an X in them. The secret message is ——— .

Mystery Word #3

WHO AM I? TIC-TAC-TOE

For one or two children

Subjects: Joseph, Isaac, Moses, Jacob, Daniel, Abraham, Elijah, Samson, Paul, Peter

Bible learning objectives: Sorting biographical information and learning about Bible characters to reinforce Bible skills.

Educational objective: Seeking information from a specific source.

Evaluation procedure: Each child checks his or her opponent's answer in the Bible before points are given. When only one child is using this activity, he or she is responsible for checking the answers with the Bible.

Materials needed:
folder, poster board, felt-tipped marker, scissors, pencil, felt

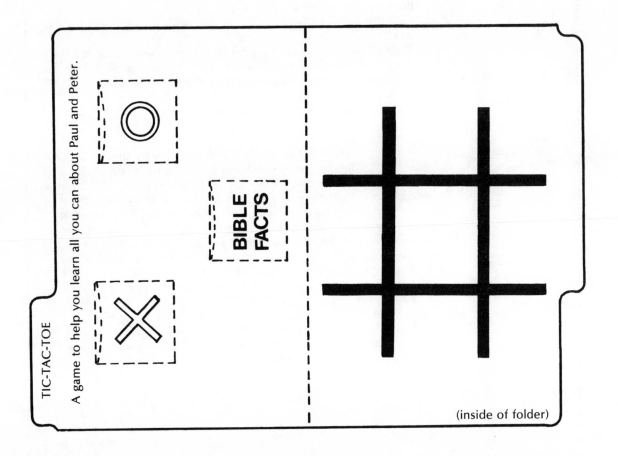

TIC-TAC-TOE

A game to help you learn all you can about Paul and Peter.

BIBLE FACTS

(inside of folder)

Directions:

1. Open the folder and draw a large Tic-Tac-Toe pattern on one side. (See diagram.)
2. Use the poster board and make fact cards, two-and-a-half inches by one-and-a-half inches, for each character. Put one fact about a Bible character on each card.
3. Use the patterns provided to make five felt X's and five felt O's.
4. Prepare the outside and inside of the folder as shown in the diagrams.
5. There are enough fact cards for six game folders included in this activity. (You can hand letter these questions on larger cards if your children need larger print for easier reading.)

TIC-TAC-TOE

Who can play:	one or two children
You will need:	Bibles, Tic-Tac-Toe game board, fact cards, felt X's and O's
How to play:	1. If two children are playing, decide who will take *(Bible name)*, and who will take *(Bible name)*. (Decide who gets the X's and who gets the O's.) 2. Take the fact cards out of the pocket and turn them face down on the table. Mix them up. 3. Take the X's and O's out of the pocket and place them in front of you. 4. The first player chooses a card, reads it, and decides if it is a Bible fact about his or her character. If it is, the card is placed on the game board in any position the player wishes. Then an X or O is placed on top of the card. 5. If it is not a fact about your character, place the card face up in front of you. In this case, you do not get to place an X or an O on the game board. 6. If it isn't your turn, look up the Scripture provided on the fact card and check to see if your opponent made the right choice. If his or her answer is incorrect, and it is your character, you may place the card on the game board. Be sure to place your marker over it. If your opponent's answer was incorrect, and it *was* his or her character, then he or she loses that turn and no one places a marker. 7. The second player may use the card lying face up in front of the other player or may draw from the mixed-up cards on the table. 8. After choosing a card, a player places it either in front of himself or herself or on the game board, while his/her opponent looks up the answer. 9. The winner is the first player with three markers in a row. 10. If you are the only player, match the cards to the names of the characters which are printed at the top of this folder. Check the answers and increase your Bible skills. *Let us do good unto all men.* (Galatians 6:10) (outside of folder)

Fact cards:

1. Sold as a slave in Egypt (Genesis 37:27, 28)	2. Forgave his brothers (Genesis 45:4-15)	3. Sons were Esau and Jacob (Genesis 25:19-26)	4. Son of Jacob (Genesis 30:24)	5. Served in the house of Potiphar (Genesis 39:1)	6. Miraculous son of Abraham (Genesis 17:15-19)
7. Possessed large flocks and herds (Genesis 26:12-14)	8. His father's favorite child (Genesis 37:3)	9. Falsely accused and cast into prison (Genesis 39)	10. Would not argue over wells of water (Genesis 26:15-22)	11. Brothers were jealous of him (Genesis 37:4-11)	12. An interpreter of dreams (Genesis 40:5-23)
13. Father told to offer him as a sacrifice (Genesis 22:1-19)	14. Jacob tricked him (Genesis 27:1-29)	15. Dreamed strange dreams (Genesis 37:5-11)	16. Made the governor of Egypt (Genesis 41:37-46)	17. Married Rebekah (Genesis 24:67)	18. Loved Esau more than Jacob (Genesis 25:28)
19. Killed an Egyptian (Exodus 2:11, 12)	20. Brother was Aaron (Exodus 4:14)	21. Deceived his father Isaac (Genesis 27:1-29)	22. Was almost blind when he was old (Genesis 27:1)	23. Married Zipporah (Exodus 2:15-22)	24. Under divine direction, brought plagues upon the land of Egypt (Exodus 7:20)
25. Dreamed about a ladder (Genesis 28:10-12)	26. Herded sheep for his father-in-law (Exodus 3:1)	27. Twin born last (Genesis 25:24-26)	28. God confirmed His covenant with Abraham to him (Genesis 28:13-22)	29. Hidden in an ark when a baby (Exodus 2:3-10)	30. Saw a burning bush (Exodus 3:2-6)
31. Twin brother of Esau (Genesis 25:24-26)	32. Worked 14 years for Leah and Rachel (Genesis 29:15-30)	33. Adopted by Pharaoh's daughter (Exodus 2:5-10)	34. God made him leader of the Israelites (Exodus 3:10-22)	35. Name was changed to Israel (Genesis 32:28)	36. Educated in the king's court (Daniel 1:19-21)
37. King Nebuchadnezzar was pleased with his knowledge (Daniel 1:18, 19)	38. Let Lot have first choice (Genesis 13:8, 9)	39. Wrestled with an angel (Genesis 32:24)	40. Interpreted dream (Daniel 2:16)	41. Prayed three times a day (Daniel 6:10)	42. Made a covenant with God (Genesis 15)

Fact cards:

43. Had 12 sons (Genesis 35:22-26)	44. Thrown into the lions' den (Daniel 6)	45. God revealed prophecy to him (Daniel 12:4)	46. Name was changed from Abram (Genesis 17:5)	47. Jewish captive in Babylon (Daniel 1:8)	48. Wouldn't eat the king's meat (Daniel 1:8)
49. Married Sarah (Genesis 11:29)	50. Angels appeared to him (Genesis 18:1-16)	51. Also called Belteshazzar (Daniel 1:7)	52. Friends were Shadrach, Meshach, and Abednego (Daniel 1:7)	53. Moved to Haran (Genesis 11:31)	54. Ishmael was his son (Genesis 16:15)
55. Killed a lion and a bear (1 Samuel 17:34-36)	56. Fought and defeated many Philistines (1 Samuel 18:6-9)	57. Fed by ravens (1 Kings 17:1-7)	58. Son was Isaac (Genesis 21:3)	59. Anointed king while still a boy (1 Samuel 16:13)	60. Solomon was his son (1 Kings 1:11-14)
61. God told him to go to Zarephath (1 Kings 17:8-16)	62. God told him to sacrifice Isaac (Genesis 22:1-19)	63. Armor bearer and musician in Saul's court (1 Samuel 16:18-23)	64. Wanted to build a temple to God (2 Samuel 7:1-17)	65. Challenged the prophets of Baal (1 Kings 18:20-29)	66. Canaan given to him and his descendants (Genesis 12:1-7)
67. Killed Goliath (1 Samuel 17)	68. Wrote Psalm 23	69. Killed the prophets of Baal (1 Kings 18:40)	70. Saul was jealous of him (1 Samuel 18:8-30)	71. Loved Jonathan (1 Samuel 18:1-4)	72. A prophet persecuted by Ahab (1 Kings 17:1-4)
73. Jezebel tried to kill him (1 Kings 19:1-18)	74. A judge of Israel (Judges 16:28-31)	75. Appointed Elisha to be prophet after him (1 Kings 19:19-21)	76. A Nazarite (Judges 13:2-7, 24)	77. Appeared to Jesus at the transfiguration (Matthew 17:3, 4)	78. Killed a lion (Judges 14:5, 6)
79. Prayed for rain after drought (1 Kings 18:41-45)	80. Killed 1000 Philistines with a jawbone (Judges 15:15, 16)	81. Foretold a drought to Ahab (1 Kings 17:1)	82. Very strong (Judges 15:9-14)	83. Told a riddle (Judges 14:12-14)	84. Saw Stephen stoned (Acts 8:1)

85. Gamaliel was his teacher (Acts 22:3)

86. Loved a Philistine woman named Delilah (Judges 16:1-20)

87. Apostle (Romans 1:1)

88. Persecuted Christians (Acts 8:3)

89. A Jew (Acts 22:3)

90. Blinded by the Philistines (Judges 16:20, 21)

91. Born in Tarsus (Acts 9:11)

92. Blinded on the Damascus road (Acts 9:3-9)

93. A fisherman (Matthew 4:18)

94. Was never to cut his hair (Judges 13:5, 24)

95. Also called Saul (Acts 13:9)

96. Wrote the book of Romans (1:1)

97. Also called Simon (Matthew 16:16-19)

98. Angel announced his birth (Judges 13:2, 3, 24)

99. A Roman citizen (Acts 16:37)

100. Shipwrecked, imprisoned, beaten (2 Corinthians 11:23-27)

101. Mother-in-law healed by Jesus (Matthew 8:14-16)

102. An apostle (Matthew 10:2)

103. Denied Jesus three times (Matthew 26:69-75)

104. Wrote two epistles of the New Testament (1 Peter 1:1) (2 Peter 1:1)

105. Followed Jesus the night He was arrested (Matthew 26:58)

106. Walked on the water to Jesus (Matthew 14:28-31)

107. Jesus told him, "Feed my sheep." (John 21:15-17)

108. Cut off the ear of Malchus (John 18:10)

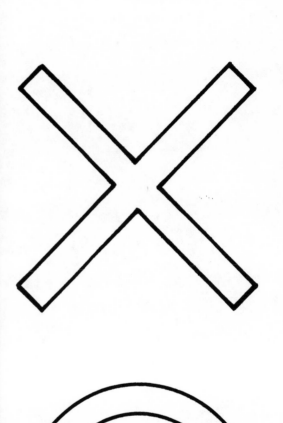

BIBLE COVER-UP

For one or more children

Subjects: Barnabas, Peter, Paul, Samson, Moses, Jacob, Joseph, Isaac, Daniel, Abraham, David, and Elijah

Bible learning objective: Learning facts about Bible characters.

Educational objective: Reading a Bible passage to gain specific information.

Evaluation procedure: Each child checks his or her opponent's answer in the Bible before points are given.

Materials needed:
   folder, ruler, poster board, sponge, felt-tipped marker

Directions:

1. Open the folder and transfer the game board to the inside. Make a number cube out of the sponge. (See p. 14)

2. Make twenty-five poster board cards, one and one-fourth by one and three-

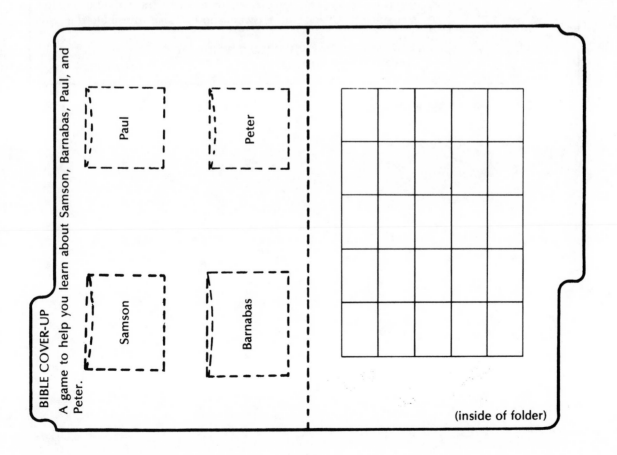

fourths inches. Type or print one Bible name on each card. (Or cut out small cards provided.)

3. Prepare the inside and outside of the folder as shown in the diagrams.
4. Three game boards are provided in this activity.

BIBLE COVER-UP	
Who can play:	one or more children
You will need:	game board, Bible name cards, numbered cube, score paper, pencil, Bible
How to play:	1. Throw the cube. The player with the highest number plays first. 2. When your turn comes, you may choose a card from any of the pockets and cover any square that you think describes that Bible character. 3. If it is *not* your turn, you must look up the Scripture to see if your opponent has chosen the correct square. 4. If a player chooses the correct square, he or she gets 200 points. 5. If a player does not choose the correct square, the player who looked up the Scripture gets 100 points and may place the name on the correct square. 6. When all of the squares are matched to name cards, add up your points to see who won the game. 7. If you are the only person playing, try to match the name cards to the fact squares. Check your answers and increase your Bible skills. *Hear instruction, and be wise, and refuse it not.* (Proverbs 8:33) <div align="right">(outside of folder)</div>

1. Killed a lion and a bear (1 Samuel 17:34-36)

2. A prophet persecuted by Ahab (1 Kings 17:1-4)

3. Fed by ravens (1 Kings 17:1-7)

4. Jewish captive in Babylon (Daniel 1:8)

5. Married Sarah (Genesis 11:29)

6. Also called Belteshazzar (Daniel 1:7)

7. Moved to Haran (Genesis 11:31)

8. Let Lot have first choice (Genesis 13)

9. Was anointed king while still a boy (1 Samuel 16:13)

10. Challenged the prophets of Baal (1 Kings 18:20-29)

11. Jezebel tried to kill him (1 Kings 19:1-18)

12. Saul was jealous of him (1 Samuel 18:8-30)

13. Friends were Shadrach, Meshach, Abednego (Daniel 1:7)

14. Name was changed from Abram (Genesis 17:5)

15. Angels appeared to him (Genesis 18:1-16)

16. Ishmael was his son (Genesis 16:15)

17. Prayed three times a day (Daniel 6:10)

18. God revealed prophecy to him (Daniel 12:4)

19. Treated Mephibosheth with kindness (2 Samuel 9:6, 7)

20. Appeared to Jesus at the transfiguration (Matthew 17:3, 4)

21. Solomon was his son (1 Kings 1:11-14)

22. Prayed for rain after drought (1 Kings 18:41-45)

23. Wrote Psalm 23

24. Wanted to build a temple for God (2 Samuel 7:1-17)

25. Wouldn't eat the king's meat (Daniel 1:8)

1. Son of Jacob (Genesis 30:24)	2. Miraculous son of Abraham (Genesis 17:15-19)	3. Married Rebekah (Genesis 24:67)	4. A Levite (Exodus 2:1-10)	5. Son of Isaac (Genesis 25:24-26)
6. Hidden in an ark (Exodus 2:3-10)	7. Twin brother of Esau (Genesis 25:24-26)	8. Falsely accused and cast into prison (Genesis 39)	9. An interpreter of dreams (Genesis 40:5-23)	10. Lived 180 years (Genesis 35:28)
11. Forgave his brothers (Genesis 45:4-15)	12. Sold as a slave in Egypt (Genesis 37:27, 28)	13. Sons were Esau and Jacob (Genesis 25:19-26)	14. Possessed large flocks and herds (Genesis 26:12-14)	15. Dreamed about a ladder (Genesis 28:10-12)
16. Deceived his father Isaac (Genesis 27:1-29)	17. His brother was Aaron (Exodus 4:14)	18. Led the people across the Red Sea (Exodus 14:21, 22)	19. Worked 14 years for Leah and Rachel (Genesis 29:15-30)	20. Saw a burning bush (Exodus 3:2-6)
21. Wrestled with an angel (Genesis 32:24)	22. Received the Ten Commandments from God (Exodus 19, 20)	23. Loved Esau more than Jacob (Genesis 25:28)	24. Had 12 sons (Genesis 35:23-26)	25. Adopted by Pharaoh's daughter (Exodus 2:5-10)

Game board # 3 (Barnabas, Peter, Paul, Samson)

1. Apostle (Romans 1:1)	6. A Levite (Acts 4:36, 37)	11. Also called Simon (Matthew 16:16-19)	16. The people thought he was the god Jupiter (Acts 14:12)	21. Walked on the water to Jesus (Matthew 14:28-31)
2. Born in Tarsus (Acts 9:11)	7. Gave his possessions to share with the other disciples (Acts 4:36, 37)	12. Mother-in-law healed by Jesus (Matthew 8:14-16)	17. He was very strong (Judges 15:12-14)	22. Gamaliel was his teacher (Acts 22:3)
3. A fisherman (Matthew 4:18)	8. A Nazarite (Judges 13:2-7, 24)	13. Killed 1000 Philistines with a jaw-bone (Judges 15:15, 16)	18. Wrote the book of Romans (1:1)	23. He wasn't to cut his hair (Judges 13:5, 24)
4. Also called Joses (Acts 4:36)	9. Also called Saul (Acts 13:9)	14. Brought Paul to Antioch (Acts 11:25, 26)	19. Jesus told him to "Feed my sheep" (John 21:15-17)	24. Blinded on the Damascus road (Acts 9:3-9)
5. A judge of Israel (Judges 16:30, 31)	10. He persecuted Christians (Acts 8:3)	15. Preached to a king (Acts 26:1, 2)	20. Denied Jesus (Matthew 26:69-75)	25. Told a riddle (Judges 14:12-14)

Answer cards for Bible-Cover-Up game board #1:

David	Elijah	Elijah	Daniel	Abraham
Daniel	Abraham	Abraham	David	Elijah
Elijah	David	Daniel	Abraham	Abraham
Abraham	Daniel	Daniel	David	Elijah
David	Elijah	David	David	Daniel

Answer cards for Bible Cover-Up game board #2:

Joseph	Isaac	Isaac	Moses	Jacob
Moses	Jacob	Joseph	Joseph	Isaac
Joseph	Joseph	Isaac	Isaac	Jacob
Jacob	Moses	Moses	Jacob	Moses
Jacob	Moses	Isaac	Jacob	Moses

Answer cards for Bible Cover-Up game board #3:

Paul	Paul	Peter	Barnabas	Samson
Paul	Barnabas	Samson	Paul	Paul
Peter	Peter	Samson	Barnabas	Paul
Barnabas	Samson	Paul	Peter	Peter
Peter	Paul	Samson	Paul	Samson

PUZZLES

For any number of children
Subject: General
Bible learning objective: Becoming more familiar with the Bible.
Educational objective: Categorizing information.
Evaluation procedure: Check sheets.

Materials needed:
   one and one-half folders, pencils, work sheets

Directions:
1. Prepare the inside and outside of the folder, and the insertion, as shown in the diagrams.
2. Duplicate the work sheets. Make an answer check sheet for each one.

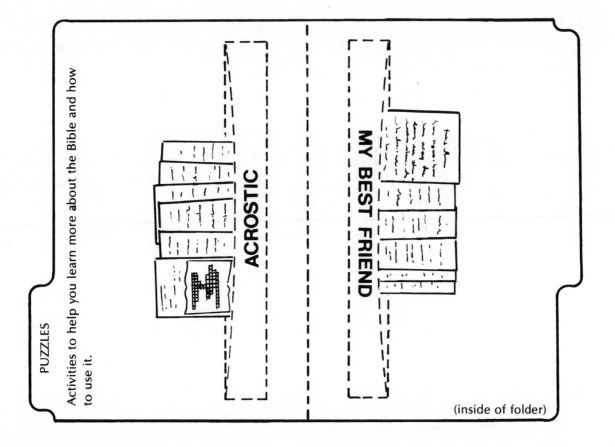

PUZZLES

Activities to help you learn more about the Bible and how to use it.

ACROSTIC

MY BEST FRIEND

(inside of folder)

Extension:

Many varieties of this folder can be made from your regular Sunday-school materials, take-home papers, and classroom activities. When you find a puzzle or acrostic that might be suitable, work it up into a folder such as this, label it, and file for future use.

PUZZLES

Who can use:	anyone
You will need:	work sheets, Bibles, pencils
How to use:	1. Choose a puzzle you would like to work. 2. Use your Bible to help you find the words. 3. Check your answers by using the check sheet.

Check Sheets for Puzzles

Thy word is true from the beginning. (Psalm 119:160)

(outside of folder)

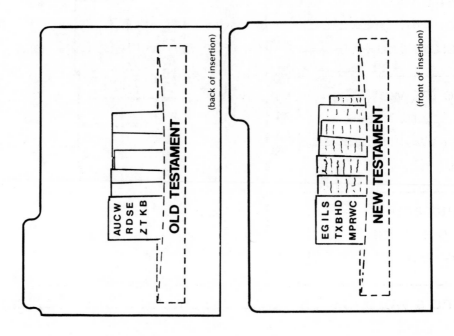

(back of insertion)

AUCW
RDSE
ZT KB

OLD TESTAMENT

(front of insertion)

EGILS
TXBHD
MPRWC

NEW TESTAMENT

Word Find:

```
Z W X A B W O R K E T H C P H
N I P M O A C T H P R O N I E
N T E R I L G E H V B I O T R
H S T D G H A T O Y N C E D G
R A M F M I H W G S D L O V E
W O V T A S V E S E L F E D A
P E R B L P I L L M J E S U S
```

My Best Friend Puzzle

1. Count five rows down. Write the letters in the last four squares.
2. Count down seven rows. Write the letters in the seventh, eighth, and ninth columns across.
3. Starting with the sixth column across, write a seven-letter word.
4. Count three rows down. Write the word made with every other letter in that row.
5. Count five rows down and seven columns across. Reading backward, write a word that means a person.
6. Look in the second and third rows down and find a two-letter word meaning the opposite of yes.
7. Look in the fourth row down and eighth and ninth rows across and find a two-letter word that sounds like two.

Write the words you found here._____

Unscramble the words to write a Bible verse found in Romans 13:10.

8. Find another verse about neighbors in the word find. Use three words you have already found. (The answer is in the last part of Mark 12:33.)

9. Find a word that tells you the name of your best friend.

Fill in the acrostic to find out who wrote these books of the New Testament:

1. The eleventh book of the New Testament.
2. The nineteenth book of the New Testament.
3. The ninth book of the New Testament.
4. The thirteenth book of the New Testament.
5. The fourteenth book of the New Testament.
6. The eighth book of the New Testament.
7. The sixth book of the New Testament.
8. The seventh book of the New Testament.
9. The fifteenth and sixteenth books of the New Testament.
10. The tenth book of the New Testament.
11. The twelfth book of the New Testament.
12. The seventeenth book of the New Testament.
13. The eighteenth book of the New Testament.

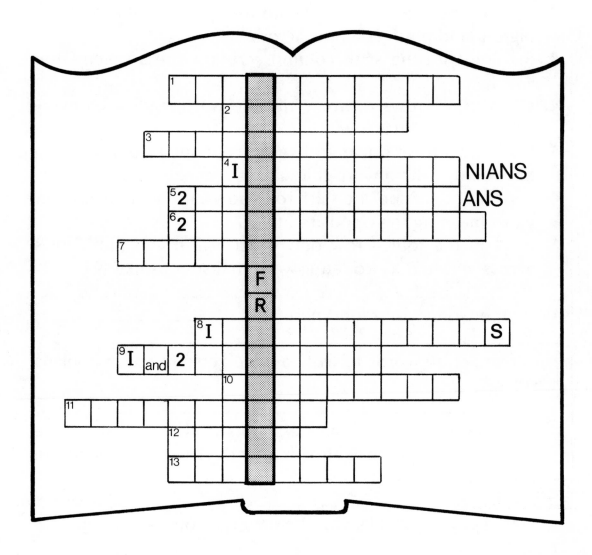

```
R E V E L A T I O N S R N K
Z N W X A B I W O T E O E E
Y H T O M I T U C O M N D I
P O R H T A U A C E A U C O
H J I T R H S T L K J C O M
I O B V H N E I G U L S R I
L E D G A N H T H L E N I R
I C N M Y P E T E R U A N O
P A O R H S T D B H A I T T
P R M F S I M A R K H T H W
I A V E L F E A E D S A I G
A T M A T T H E W O P L A E
N L R B C O L O S S I A N S
S E P H E S I A N S M G S Q
S N A I N O L A S S E H T S
```

Find and circle the names of the books of the New Testament.

```
H T E R E H T S E B G F V I E O R
E L D B I E P R O V E R B S P U T
L S B E Z E K I E L N H N I S T O
J O S H U S U D O X E D A N I E L
U L D O L T S J R B S O H O S S Z
D O S S A L E V I T I C U S A E E
G M E E M R T R O R S D M E I T P
E O L A E H S J O N A H R F A S H
S N C M N A O K E N O U L C H A A
C S I S T B B I Z W O U E M I I N
K A N R A N A N E H E M I A H S I
H M O E T A D G K T Z T Y E C E A
A U R B I H I S B U R G S N A L H
C E H M O P A U O R A J O E L C R
I L C U N E H C P S A L M S A C K
M I H N S Z E C H A R I A H M E P
T H I A G G A H A B A K K U K R Q
Y B F P E S J O S H U A H N F O B
```

Find and circle the names of the books of the Old Testament.

JERUSALEM TO JERICHO

For two children

Subject: The good Samaritan

Bible learning objectives: Learning the principles of the parable of the good Samaritan and how to apply them to our personal lives.

Educational objectives: Being responsible for seeking out specific information and committing it to memory.

Evaluation procedure: Each child checks opponent's answers in the Bible before points are given.

Materials needed:
folder, poster board, foam rubber cube, button markers (2), crayons or felt-tipped markers

---

Directions:

1. Open the folder and transfer the game board to the inside of the folder. (See diagram.) Color the pictures and path with crayons or markers.

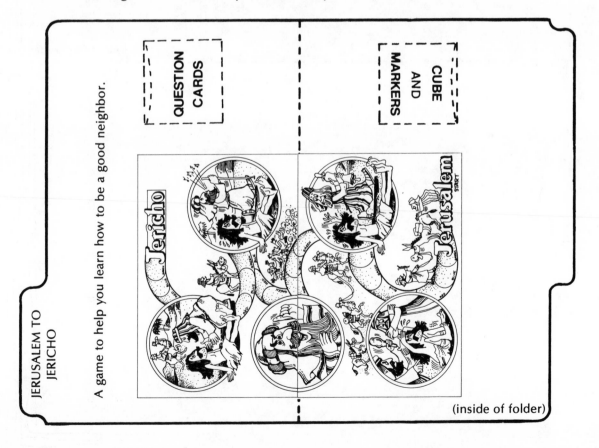

(inside of folder)

2. Prepare the outside of the folder as shown in the diagram.
3. Color two sides of a foam cube blue, two sides green, and two sides red.
4. Make fifteen question cards, two inches by two inches.

JERUSALEM TO JERICHO	
Who can play:	two children
You will need:	game board, colored cube, two button markers, question cards, Bibles
How to play:	1. Decide who will play first. 2. The first player chooses a question card and answers the question. 3. If it is not your turn, look up the Scripture on the question card to check the answer given by your opponent. (If your opponent answered incorrectly, then you may advance one place.) 4. If the answer is correct, the player throws the colored cube, moves to the color indicated, and follows the directions on that color. 5. If there are no directions, the player's turn is over. 6. All large circles count for one space. 7. The first player to reach Jericho is the winner. *Thou shalt love thy neighbor as thyself.* (Matthew 22:39) (outside of folder)

Jericho

Samaritan pays innkeeper.
(Go to Jericho)

Levite walks on by without helping.
(Go back two spaces)

Samaritan stops.
(Throw again)

Rock slide.
(Jump ahead one space)

Samaritan helps you.
(Go ahead two spaces)

Levite looks at you.
(Go back one space)

RED   BLUE   GREEN
RED   BLUE   GREEN   BLUE
GREEN   RED

Lap the other part of the game board over this flap and glue.

Jerusalem START

Priest passes by on the other side. (Go back one space)

God loves you. (Move ahead two spaces)

Give donkey a carrot. (Move ahead one space)

Bandits. (Lose one turn)

GREEN
BLUE
RED

83

Question cards:

1. What did Jesus tell the young man he had to do to live eternally? (Luke 10:27, 28)	2. What did the priest do? (Luke 10:31)	3. Who was the third man who came down the road to Jericho? (Luke 10:33)
4. Who asked Jesus what he had to do to inherit eternal life? (Luke 10:25)	5. What did Jesus ask the lawyer after he told the story of the good Samaritan? (Luke 10:36)	6. Where did the man in Jesus' story begin his journey? (Luke 10:30)
7. What did the Samaritan tell the innkeeper? (Luke 10:35)	8. Who was the second man who saw the wounded stranger? (Luke 10:32)	9. What did Jesus tell the lawyer to do? (Luke 10:37)
10. "Thou shalt love the Lord thy God with all thy _____, and with all thy _____ . . . and thy _____ as thyself." (Luke 10:27)	11. What did the Samaritan do when he saw the man lying beside the road? (Luke 10:34)	12. What happened to the traveler in Jesus' story? (Luke 10:30)
13. How did the Samaritan take care of the sick man? (Luke 10:34)	14. Who was first to come by and see the wounded man? (Luke 10:31)	15. What did the lawyer ask Jesus about neighbors? (Luke 10:29)

BALLOON FILL-INS

For any number of children
Subject: Concept of neighbors
Bible learning objective: Seeing practical applications of the parable of the good Samaritan.
Educational objective: Developing acceptable social and moral behavioral patterns.
Evaluation procedure: Evaluation is provided when the children share their work with the group during a discussion period.

Materials needed:
folder, magazines, crayons or felt-tipped markers, pencils, paper, Bibles

Directions:
1. Make four pockets and position them on the inside of the folder and on an extra insertion to the folder as shown in the one example diagram.

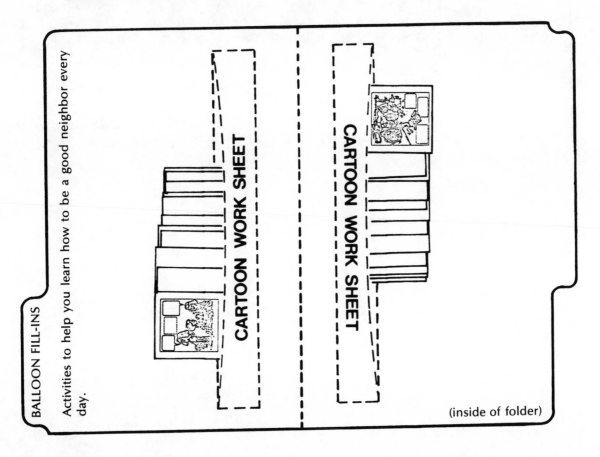

(inside of folder)

2. Prepare the outside of the folder as shown in the diagram.
3. Provide the four cartoon work sheets. Duplicate them or laminate. (If you provide individual copies, they can also be colored. The laminated sheets can be marked with a grease pencil by the children, then erased and used over and over again.)

Extension:

Other folders can be made by finding appropriate magazine pictures or cartoons from a newspaper. Mount them on the inside of folders and draw the Scripture and speech balloons.

If you laminate these sheets and provide a grease pencil, they can be used over and over again. However, individual copies do provide an extra activity for those children who like to color.

Encourage the children to draw a more satisfying conclusion for the cartoons. Be sure to provide paper and pencils for their masterpieces.

BALLOON FILL-INS

Who can use:	anyone
You will need:	cartoon work sheets, crayons, pencils, Bibles
How to use:	1. Choose a cartoon work sheet from the folder. 2. Read and follow the instructions at the bottom of the work sheet. *A new commandment I give unto you, That ye love one another; as I have loved you.* (John 13:34) (outside of folder)

To find out how God would want you to act in this situation, look up Proverbs 17:17 and write it in the thought balloon with the dotted lines. Write the conversation you imagine in the balloons with the solid lines.

To find out how God would want you to act in this situation, look up Luke 6:31 and write it in the thought balloon with the dotted lines. Write the conversation you imagine in the balloons with the solid lines.

To find out how God would want you to act in this situation, look up Galatians 6:10 and write it in the thought balloon with the dotted lines. Write the conversation you imagine in the balloon with the solid lines.

To find out how God would want you to act in this situation, look up Romans 13:10 or Ephesians 4:32 and write it in the thought balloon with the dotted lines. Write the conversation you imagine in the balloons with the solid lines.

CLASS PHOTOGRAPH ALBUM

For any number of children
Subject: Loving our neighbors
Bible learning objective: Learning to love others and ourselves.
Educational objective: Helping children to become aware of others and their own personal worth.
Evaluation procedure: The entire project is a personal evaluation.

> **Materials needed:**
> folder, work sheet, pencils, camera

Directions:
1. Open the folder and make one pocket for the work sheet.
2. Decorate the other side of the folder with pictures of things children like to do. Include pictures of church attendance, reading the Bible, and singing

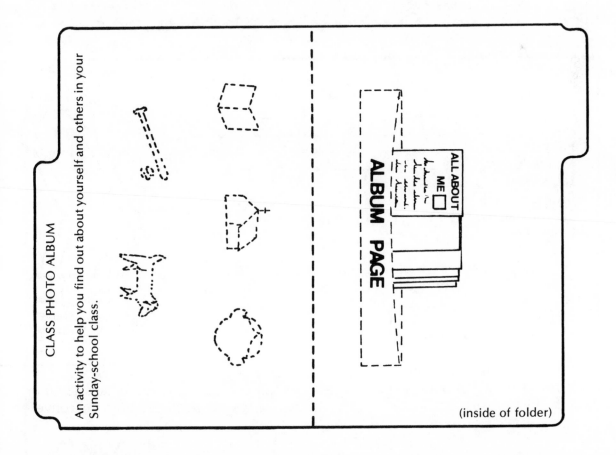

CLASS PHOTO ALBUM

An activity to help you find out about yourself and others in your Sunday-school class.

ALBUM PAGE

ALL ABOUT ME

(inside of folder)

hymns, as well as everyday activities.
3. Prepare the outside of the folder as shown in the diagram.

Extension:

Let the children prepare an album for the staff members of the church. Share the different pages with the children as a group by featuring one child per week.

Take Polaroid pictures of new members and let them add a page to the book. This will help them feel an immediate sense of belonging.

Make the finished book available to the children each Sunday.

CLASS PHOTO ALBUM

Who can use:	anyone
You will need:	work sheet, pencil
How to use:	1. Fill out the work sheet. 2. Share your work sheet with friends during discussion time. *If God so loved us, we ought also to love one another.* (1 John 4:11)

(outside of folder)

ALL ABOUT ME

Name _____
Address _____
Phone _____
Mother's name _____
Father's name _____
Brothers' names _____
Sisters' names _____
Kind of pet _____ Name of pet _____

Where I go to school _____
Grade _____ Favorite subject _____
Favorite Bible story _____
One way I try to please God _____
My favorite Bible verse _____
_____
What I like best about Sunday school _____
What I like best about my church _____
Why I love Jesus _____
_____

WHO IS MY NEIGHBOR?

For two to ten children
Subject: Golden Rule
Bible learning objective: Discovering ways to help one another as Jesus instructed.
Educational objective: Learning how to get along with others.
Evaluation procedure: Discussion with peers.

Materials needed:
 folder, marker, foam cube, mystery envelope, poster board, construction paper, straight pins

Directions:
1. Open the folder and transfer the game board.
2. Type this mystery message on a card and place it in the envelope: When people obey the Golden Rule, "Do to others what you would have them do to you," Matthew 7:12, EVERYBODY WINS!

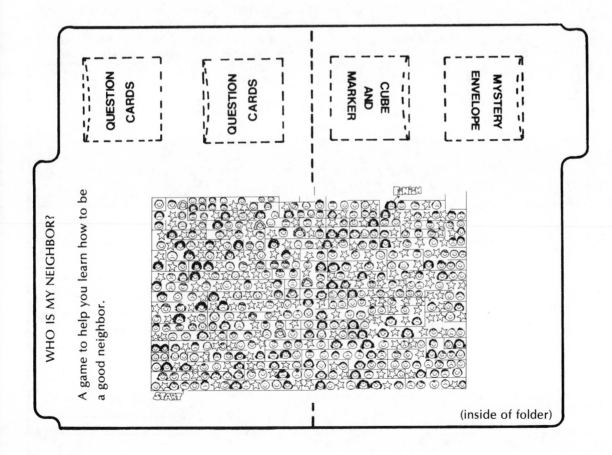

(inside of folder)

3. Use the pattern provided and make "Everybody Wins" buttons for each child who plays the game. Put a straight pin through each one and place it in the mystery envelope. (If you prefer not to use pins, masking tape works well, too.)
4. Cut out the question strips and glue them to five inch by three-fourths inch poster board.
5. Prepare the inside and outside of the folder as shown in the diagrams.

WHO IS MY NEIGHBOR?	
Who can play:	two to ten children
You will need:	maze game board, one marker, questions, numbered cube, mystery envelope
How to play:	1. Everybody uses the same marker. 2. The first player throws the cube and moves the marker in the direction he or she thinks leads out of the maze. 3. If you land on a star, move ahead one free space. 4. If you land on a face with a smile, pick a question from the envelope with the smiling face and answer the question on the card. 5. If you land on a face with a frown, choose a question from the envelope with the frowning face. You must rephrase the statement so it wouldn't hurt someone's feelings, or you can tell how you could change yourself so someone wouldn't feel he or she had to make that statement to you. 6. If you see your neighbors going in the wrong direction on the game board, you may quietly raise your hand and help them (with a smile). You may also help a player answer the question in a quiet and pleasant manner. Anytime you help a player, the marker can be moved an extra time. 7. When the maze is finished, you may open the mystery message and read it. 8. Each player receives an "Everybody Wins" button. *Be ye kind one to another, tenderhearted, forgiving one another.* (Ephesians 4:32) <div align="right">(outside of folder)</div>

To the teacher:

This game should be played under your direction. Guide the children with your questions but refrain from making judgments. When a child comes up with a response that is negative, you might say:

- Is this what Jesus would do?
- How would the other person feel if you said that?
- Is there any other way you could respond to that person?
- Would it be necessary to say anything, or is it sometimes best to keep silent and listen?
- Should you be a neighbor to someone who acts like that?
- Why do you suppose someone would say an ugly thing like that?
- Have you ever heard anyone say that?
- Have you ever said that?
- Why did you say it?
- How did you feel when someone said that to you?
- How do you think someone felt when they made the same statement to you?

The children should keep discussing until they come up with an answer that pleases everyone.

Make a special note of the responses of the individual children. You may learn that some children are hypersensitive, lonely, shy, or aggressive. Later on you can lead discussions and activities to help with their problems. This activity will be a lot of fun for you as well as the children.

Pattern for construction
paper pin

Question strips:

☺	How can you be a neighbor to someone who is bored?	☹	If you do that again, I'll break your head!
☺	How can you be a neighbor to someone who is worried?	☹	You drive me crazy!
☺	How can you be a neighbor to someone who is shy?	☹	Quit!
☺	How can you be a neighbor to someone who is ugly?	☹	I have to do all the work!
☺	How can you be a neighbor to someone who is critical of you?	☹	Clumsy!
☺	How can you be a neighbor to someone who is a failure?	☹	You make me sick!
☺	How can you be a neighbor to someone who is confused?	☹	It's my turn!
☺	How can you be a neighbor to someone who is angry?	☹	Get off my back!
☺	How can you be a neighbor to someone who is crying?	☹	I'm gonna get you!
☺	How can you be a neighbor to someone who hurts others?	☹	You're cheating!
☺	How can you be a neighbor to the people who live next door?	☹	Don't you ever do anything right?
☺	How can you be a neighbor to someone who hurts your feelings?	☹	Shut your face!
☺	How can you be a neighbor to someone who is destructive?	☹	You're stupid!
☺	How can you be a neighbor to someone who is mean?	☹	I'll tell on you!
☺	How can you be a neighbor to someone who isn't too smart?	☹	It's your fault!
☺	How can you be a neighbor to someone who has made a mistake	☹	You're not listening!
☺	How can you be a neighbor to someone who is frustrated?	☹	Shut up!
☺	How can you be a neighbor to someone who doesn't like you?	☹	Get out of my way!
☺	How can you be a neighbor to someone who is embarrassed?	☹	I don't get to go anywhere!
☺	How can you be a neighbor to someone you don't like?	☹	You'll be sorry!
☺	How can you be a neighbor to someone who feels unloved?	☹	You don't care how I feel!
☺	How can you be a neighbor to someone who is your best friend?	☹	I was here first!
☹	Did you hear me?	☹	Everybody else does!
☹	Leave that alone. It's mine!	☹	Get out of my room!

START

Game board

Game board

BEE ATTITUDES

For one or two children
Subject: Sermon on the Mount
Bible learning objective: Learning practical applications of the Sermon on the Mount.
Educational objectives: Finding the meanings of words and expressing them in acceptable behavior.
Evaluation procedure: Check sheet.

Materials needed:

one and one-half folders, tagboard, felt-tipped markers, rubber cement, *King James and Living Bibles,* dictionary, Bible dictionary

---

Directions:

1. Open the folder and trace eight hives. (Pattern provided.) Write the verses on the hives, leaving blank spaces for the missing words.

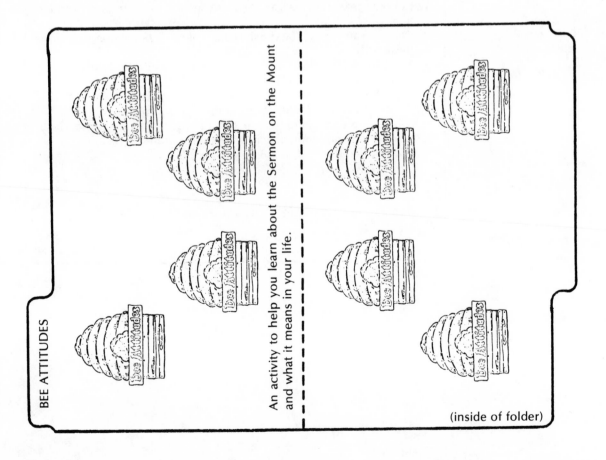

BEE ATTITUDES

An activity to help you learn about the Sermon on the Mount and what it means in your life.

(inside of folder)

2. Make eight bees from the tagboard. (Pattern provided.) Write the missing words on their wings: merciful, mourn, meek, pure in heart, peacemakers, poor in spirit, righteousness' sake, hunger and thirst.
3. Attach a small piece of velcro to the back of each bee and to each hive making sure the words on each bee will finish a verse on one hive when the bee is in place.
4. Make eight signs to fit the front of the hives. The tagboard signs should be one inch by two inches. Write one of the statements given, on each sign. Attach a piece of velcro to each sign and to the front bottom of each hive. (Pattern provided.)
5. Duplicate the work sheets.
6. Prepare the outside and inside of the folder as shown in the diagrams.
7. Cut one folder in half and prepare as the insertion diagram suggests.
8. Prepare a check sheet.

BEE ATTITUDES

Who can use:	Any number can do the work sheets. (Take turns with the bees.)
You will need:	pencil, Bible dictionary, *Webster's Dictionary*, *King James Bible*, *Living Bible*, work sheets, bees, hives, signs
How to use:	1. Get out the work sheets and read the instructions. Answer the questions. 2. Check your work sheet with the check sheet when you have finished. 3. Take the bees and the signs from the pockets of the folder. 4. Read the verses on the hives. 5. Look through the bees until you find the words that would best fill in the blanks and attach the bees in their proper places. 6. Look at the signs. Find the one that best describes the person Jesus was talking about and attach it to the front of each hive. 7. Use your work sheet to check your work. *Teach me to do thy will; for thou art my God.* (Psalm 143:10) (outside of folder)

106

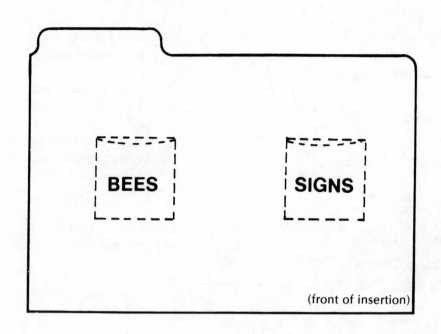

(front of insertion)

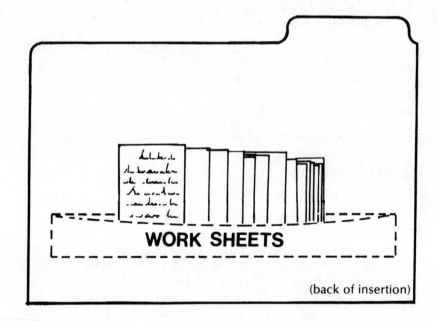

WORK SHEETS

(back of insertion)

Words to be used to fill in the blanks are:

poor in spirit	humble	proud	not proud
clean thoughts	merciful	love	kind
right desires	tenderhearted	forgiving	sin
mourn	sad	sorrow	repent
hunger and thirst	to be sorry	meek	depend on God
righteousness	just	good	satisfied
thoughts	desires	pure in heart	peacemakers
fight	quarrel	persecuted	mean
cruel			

(You can use some of the words more than one time.)

The signs should read:

1. Those who are not proud, who know they have sinned.
2. Those who are sorry for their sins.
3. Those who depend on God.
4. Those who want to be good.
5. Those who are kind, tenderhearted, and forgiving.
6. Those who have love in their hearts.
7. Those who don't quarrel, fuss, and fight.
8. Those who are treated mean and cruel because they are good.

The hives should read:

1. "Blessed are the _____ _____ _____: for theirs is the kingdom of heaven."
2. "Blessed are they that _____: for they shall be comforted."
3. "Blessed are the _____: for they shall inherit the earth."
4. "Blessed are they which do _____ _____ _____ after righteousness: for they shall be filled."
5. "Blessed are the _____: for they shall obtain mercy."
6. "Blessed are the _____ _____ _____: for they shall see God."
7. "Blessed are the _____: for they shall be called the children of God."
8. "Blessed are they which are persecuted for _____ _____: for theirs is the kingdom of heaven."

BEE ATTITUDES WORK SHEET

I. Open a *King James Bible* to Matthew 5:3-12.

   1. Read Matthew 5:3 and fill in the blanks: "Blessed are the _____ _____ _____ : for theirs is the kingdom of heaven."
   2. Read Matthew 5:3 in the *Living Bible* and fill in the blank: "_____ men are very fortunate!" he told them, "for the kingdom of heaven is given to them."
   3. Look up humble in the dictionary. Humble means not _____ .
   4. Another way of saying Matthew 5:3 might be: Blessed are those who are not _____ : for theirs is the kingdom of Heaven.
   5. Read Psalm 51:2 in the *King James Bible*. "Wash me thoroughly from mine iniquity, and cleanse me from my _____ ."
   6. Place your answer for #5 in Matthew 5:3: "Blessed are those who know they _____ : for theirs is the kingdom of heaven."

II. Read Matthew 5:4 in the *King James Bible*.

   1. "Blessed are they that _____ : for they shall be comforted."
   2. Look up mourn in the Bible dictionary. Mourn means to be _____ or to show _____ .
   3. Read Psalm 51:13 in the *Living Bible* and complete this verse: "Then I will teach your ways to other sinners, and they—guilty like me—will _____ and return to you."
   4. Look up repent in the Bible dictionary. It means _____ _____ .
   5. Put your answer for #4 in the blank spaces for Matthew 5:4: "Blessed are they that _____ for they shall be comforted."

III. Read Matthew 5:5 in the *King James Bible*.

   1. "Blessed are the _____ : for they shall inherit the earth."
   2. Look up meek in the Bible dictionary. Meek means people who _____ on _____ instead of themselves.
   3. Insert the answer for #2 in Matthew 5:5: "Blessed are those who _____ on _____ : for they shall inherit the earth."

IV. Read Matthew 5:6 in the *King James Bible*.

   1. "Blessed are they which do _____ and _____ after _____ : for they shall be filled."
   2. Read Matthew 5:6 in the *Living Bible*: "Happy are those who long to be _____ and _____ , for they shall be completely satisfied."
   3. Read Psalm 51:10 in the *Living Bible*: "Create in me a new, clean heart, O God, filled with clean _____ and _____ desires."
   4. Use the last part of #3 to fill in the blanks: "Blessed are those who want to be filled with _____ _____ for they shall be filled."

V. Read Matthew 5:7 in the *King James Bible*.

    1. "Blessed are the _____ : for they shall obtain mercy."

    2. Look up mercy in the Bible dictionary. Mercy means feelings of _____ , sympathy, and forgiveness.

    3. Read Ephesians 4:32 in the *King James Bible:* "And be ye _____ one to another, _____ , _____ one another, even as God for Christ's sake hath forgiven you."

    4. Use the words from #3 to say Matthew 5:7 another way: Blessed are they who are _____ , _____ and _____ : for they shall obtain mercy.

VI. Read Matthew 5:8 in the *King James Bible*.

    1. "Blessed are the _____ _____ _____ : for they shall see God."

    2. Read Romans 12:9 in the *Living Bible:* "Don't just pretend that you _____ others: really _____ them. Hate what is wrong. Stand on the side of the _____ ."

    3. Read 1 Peter 1:22 in the *Living Bible:* "Now you can have real _____ for everyone because your souls have been cleansed from selfishness and hatred when you trusted Christ to save you."

    4. Write the answer for #3 in Matthew 5:8 to say that verse another way: Blessed are those who have _____ in their hearts, for they shall see God.

VII. Read Matthew 5:9 in the *King James Bible*.

    1. "Blessed are the _____ : for they shall be called the children of God."

    2. Read Proverbs 20:3 in the *Living Bible:* "It is an honor for a man to stay out of a _____ ."

    3. Read Romans 12:18 in the *Living Bible:* "Don't _____ with anyone. Be at peace with everyone."

    4. Use the answers for #2 and #3 to say Matthew 5:9 another way: Blessed are those who do not _____ and _____ : for they shall be called the children of God.

VIII. Read Matthew 5:10 in the *King James Bible*.

    1. "Blessed are they which are _____ for _____ sake: for theirs is the kingdom of heaven."

    2. Read Matthew 5:10 in the *Living Bible:* "Happy are those who are persecuted because they are _____ , for the Kingdom of Heaven is theirs."

    3. Look up persecute in the Bible dictionary. Persecute means to treat someone in a _____ or _____ way, especially because he holds certain beliefs.

    4. Use the answers to #2 and #3 to make Matthew 5:10 read another way: Blessed are they which are treated in a _____ or _____ way because of righteousness' sake: for theirs is the kingdom of Heaven.

MY CHOICE

For two or more players

Subject: Making choices in everyday life that are acceptable to God

Bible learning objective: Helping children to learn Scriptures that will guide them in making choices.

Educational objective: Learning to make acceptable behavioral choices.

Evaluation procedure: Group discussion.

Materials needed:
folder, thirty-six choice cards, bell, poster board, felt-tipped marker

---

Directions:

1. Open the folder and make five pockets on the inside as shown in the diagram.
2. Label the pockets: Problems, Choices, Scriptures, No Way, and Jesus' Way.
3. Make thirty-six cards. Use a different colored poster board as backing for the problem, choice, and Scripture cards.
4. Prepare the outside of the folder as shown in the diagram.
5. You will need a little bell.

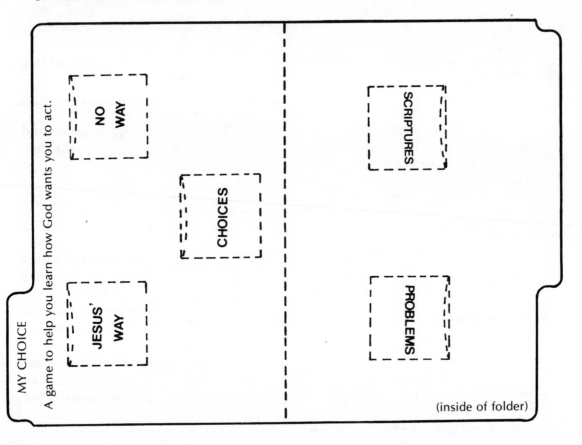

MY CHOICE

A game to help you learn how God wants you to act.

NO WAY

SCRIPTURES

CHOICES

JESUS' WAY

PROBLEMS

(inside of folder)

MY CHOICE

Who can play:	two or more players
You will need:	pocket chart (inside of folder), problem, choice, and Scripture cards, bell
How to play:	1. Scatter the choice cards on the table. Take the problem and Scripture cards from their pockets and place them in stacks underneath the pockets on the folder. 2. At the signal to go, each player takes a problem card and begins to search through the Scripture cards for a word from Jesus that might help to solve the problem "His Way." 3. When a player finds a Scripture that will help solve the problem, he or she begins to read the choice cards. There are two for each problem. One will be a right choice and one will be a wrong choice. 4. When a player thinks he or she has found a Scripture and two choice cards for a problem, the player rings the bell and says, "I need a friend to listen." 5. When any player rings the bell, all the players stop searching, fold their hands, and listen to the bell-ringer's problem and choices. 6. If the other players agree, the bell ringer places the right choice card in the pocket labeled "Jesus' Way." The wrong choice card is placed in the "No Way" pocket. 7. The signal is then given and all players return to their search until another choice is made. 8. If a player doesn't stop and listen when the bell is rung, he or she loses fifty points. 9. Those who listen properly receive one hundred points. 10. Those who make a correct match receive five hundred points. 11. The winner is the player with the most points. *Be not overcome of evil, but overcome evil with good.* (Romans 12:21) <div align="right">(outside of folder)</div>

Scripture Cards:

"Work with your own hands." (1 Thessalonians 4:11)	"Be ye kind one to another, tender-hearted, forgiving one another." (Ephesians 4:32)	"Come unto me, all ye that labor and are heavy laden, and I will give you rest." (Matthew 11:28)	"The Lord is my helper, and I will not fear." (Hebrews 13:6)
"By love serve one another." (Galatians 5:13)	"Study to show thyself approved." (2 Timothy 2:15)	"Children, obey your parents in the Lord: for this is right." (Ephesians 6:1)	"Obey them that have the rule over you." (Hebrews 13:17)
"Be not overcome of evil, but overcome evil with good." (Romans 12:21)	"Be ye doers of the word, and not hearers only." (James 1:22)	"Even a child is known by his doings." (Proverbs 20:11)	"Thou shalt not steal." (Exodus 20:15)

Choice Cards:

Talk and tease with my friends while I write cheat notes for a test.

Think of three things that make me special and give my report.

Follow Mom around the house while she's cleaning and tell her I never have any fun.

Tell my friends I need to study and excuse myself.

Pretend I'm sick that day.

Help Mom, then study my Sunday-school lesson.

Yell at Mom and slam the door when I go into my room.

Trip Billy so all the guys will like me.

Think of something good I have done and try to do better the next time.

Remember all the nice things Mom has done for me and clean my room.

Talk to Billy before class and congratulate him on the home run he hit.

Go off alone and feel sorry for myself.

Choice Cards:

Help him clean up and ask him to sit with me and my friends.

Insist that I need some extra money, even when I see the worried look on Dad's face.

Put the stickers in my pocket and walk out the door with them.

Yell, "Watch what you're doing, Clumsy!"

Enjoy the skating party, then excuse myself politely when it's time for the pizza snack.

Say, "I don't think you ought to take those." Then discuss it with my parents when I get home.

Smile and say, "You are pretty, Kyla."

Tell Mom, "I have to do everything around here!"

Count slowly to ten and do the best I can on the test.

Yell, "Look who's talking, Gorilla Face." Tell all the kids what she said.

Try to get my work done so I can do what I want.

Clown around and get in the way while the other kids are taking the test.

Problem Cards:

I watched my favorite programs on television last night and didn't study for the spelling test. Every morning I wait in the cafeteria for fifteen minutes before school starts. Usually, I talk and have fun with my friends. This morning I . . .	I'm so angry! My mother told me I couldn't go with my friend to the shopping center this afternoon because I didn't clean my room. I feel she is being unfair. I can clean my room tomorrow. She can shut the door to my room when her friends come to visit. I . . .	I have to give a report tomorrow. I always get red in the face when I have to get up in front of the class. My feet sweat and I stutter. I feel insecure, so I . . .
Billy gets up to give his report this morning. He is always so funny when he has to talk in front of the class. He gets red in the face, drops his papers, and bumps into things. Everyone laughs when it's his turn. All the guys want me to trip him when he passes my desk so he'll be really flustered. I . . .	I failed a math test this morning. At lunch, I spilled chocolate milk on my best shirt. Some of it even splashed on the most popular kid in the class. I slipped going into the library and fell flat on my face. I'm really a jerk! I . . .	It's Saturday afternoon. There is nothing good on television. My friends are all busy. It's too cold to ride my bike. There's nothing interesting to do. I . . .
This kid in my room spilled chocolate milk all over my shirt at lunch. He's really had a bad day. I know he got a failing grade on his math test. He slipped and fell in the library this morning, too. He must feel like a klutz! I . . .	A girl in our class isn't quite like the rest of us. Some of the kids call her "Retard." Sometimes she comes up to us and says stupid things that hurt our feelings. Today, she walked up to me and said, "You're ugly and I'm pretty." I . . .	The kids are all going to get pizza after the skating party tonight. I don't have enough money to go with them. I know my folks are having a rough time financially. I . . .
At our house, everyone has chores on Saturday. I watched cartoons this morning. I want to go to a movie this afternoon. Mom says I have to run the sweeper. I . . .	It's time to take the physical fitness test at school. I feel anxious because I know I'm not as good as the rest of the kids when it comes to physical activities. I . . .	I went to the store with Kelly. He picked up a neat package of Silly Stickers. I'd like to have some, too. He tells me I'm chicken if I don't put some in my pocket. I . . .

STILL THE WATERS

Two to four players or two teams

Subject: Jesus quieted the storm

Bible learning objective: Learning how Jesus dealt with His disciples's fear.

Educational objectives: Identifying times when we are afraid and developing positive action to deal with fear.

Evaluation procedure: Each player is responsible for looking up the Scriptures before any points are given for opponent's answers.

Materials needed:

one and one-half folders, button, red, yellow, green, and blue poster board, felt-tipped markers

---

Directions:

1. Open the folder and transfer the game board. Color the game board, using the same color for all 5 point spaces, another color for all 15 point, etc. (See #4) Attach the pockets as shown in the diagram.

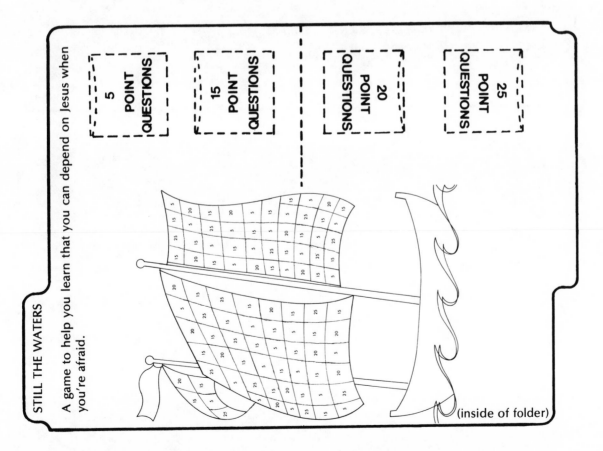

STILL THE WATERS

A game to help you learn that you can depend on Jesus when you're afraid.

5 POINT QUESTIONS

15 POINT QUESTIONS

20 POINT QUESTIONS

25 POINT QUESTIONS

(inside of folder)

2. Cut the poster board into squares one and a half inches by one and three-fourths inches.
3. Glue the questions to the back side of the poster board, and then the backs of the question cards will be in color.
4. Put the five-point questions on red, fifteen-point on blue, twenty-point on yellow, and twenty-five-point on the green poster board.

STILL THE WATERS	
Who can play:	two or four children, two teams
You will need:	game board, button, question cards, pencil, score sheet, Bible
How to play: ┌─ ─ ─ ─ ─ ┐ │ Button │ │ Marker │ └─ ─ ─ ─ ─ ┘	1. Place the game board on the edge of a table. 2. Take three small steps backward. 3. Stretch your arm over the game board and drop the button. 4. Pick out a question with the same number as the space in which most of your button fell. 5. If you answer the question, record that same number as your score. 6. The other players must check your answer in the Bible to see if it is correct. If the answer isn't correct, the first one to find the Scripture receives 10 points. 7. The first person to reach 100 points wins the game. *The Lord is my helper, and I will not fear.* (Hebrews 13:6) <div align="right">(outside of folder)</div>

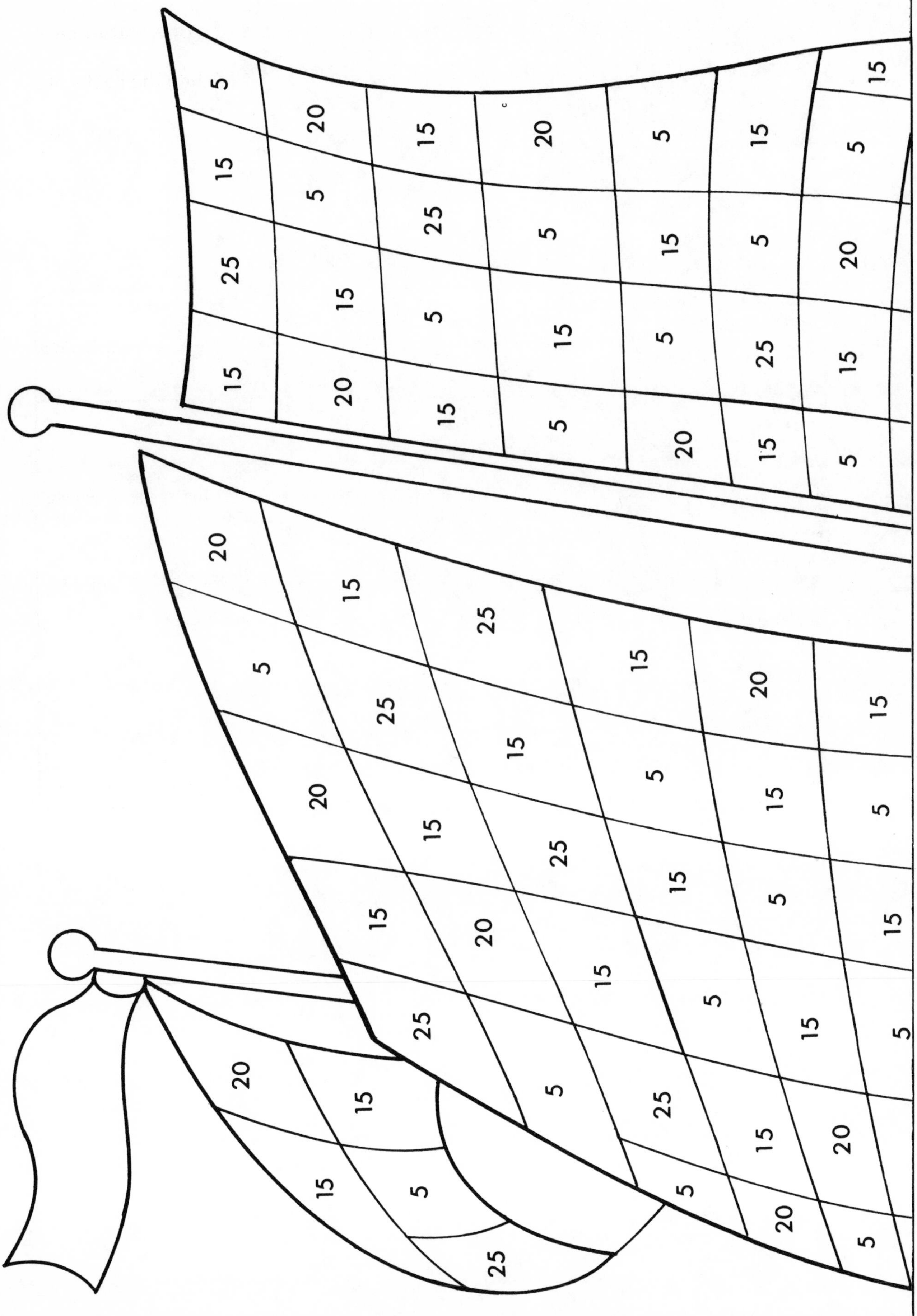
5
15
25
15
20
5
15
20
15
25
5
15
20
5
15
5
5
15
5
20
15
5
25
15
15
5
20
15
5
20
15
25
15
20
15
5
25
15
5
15
5
20
15
25
15
5
15
15
20
15
5
15
5
25
5
25
15
20
5
20
5
20
15
15
5
25

Lap the other part of the game board over this flap and glue.

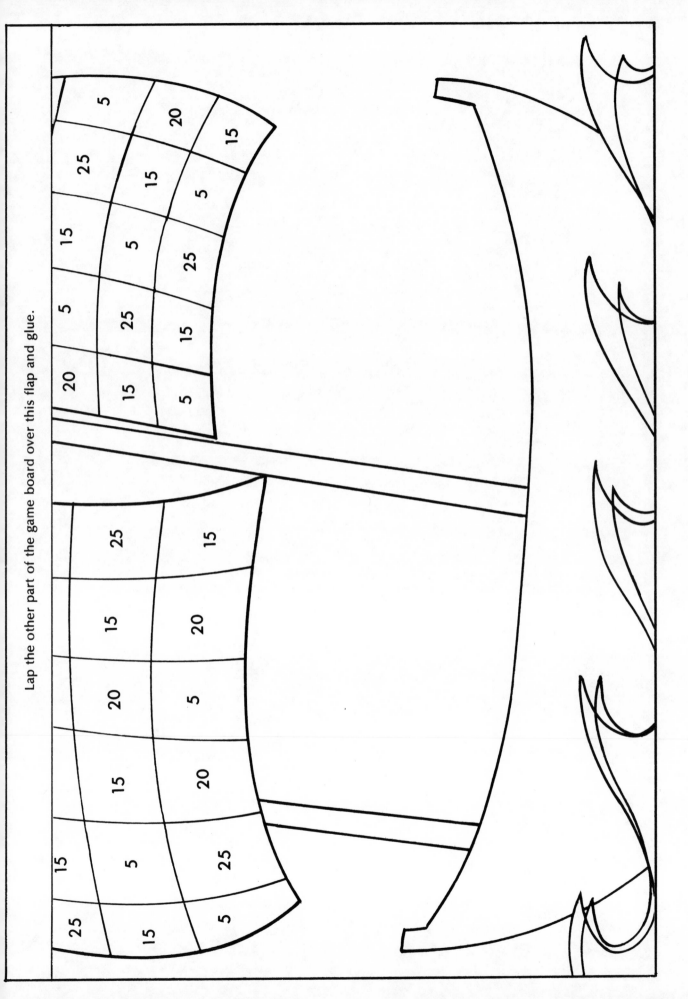

(1) What happened to the ship during the storm? (Mark 4:37) 5 points

(2) What happened when Jesus said, "Peace, be still"? (Mark 4:39) 5 points

(3) What happened while Jesus was asleep? (Luke 8:23) 5 points

(4) Why did the disciples need help? (Mark 4:37) 5 points

(5) What did Jesus say to the disciples after He stilled the water? (Mark 4:40) 15 points

(6) Who needed help from Jesus while He was asleep? (Luke 8:22) 5 points

(7) What did Jesus want to do after He taught the multitude? (Mark 4:35) 5 points

(8) What did the disciples say to Jesus when they woke Him up? (Mark 4:38) 5 points

(9) Who was with Jesus in the boat? (Luke 8:22) 15 points

(10) Where was Jesus teaching when He taught the multitudes from the boat? (Mark 4:1) 15 points

(11) What did the disciples say to one another after Jesus stilled the water? (Luke 8:25) 15 points

(12) When do I need courage? Read Psalm 31:24. It is a verse to calm the water of fear in your heart. 20 points

(13) "The Lord is my light and my salvation; whom shall I _____?" (Psalm 27:1) 20 points

(14) "God is our refuge and strength, a very present _____ in trouble." (Psalm 46:1) 25 points

(15) "The Lord is my strength and my shield; my heart trusted in him, and I am _____." (Psalm 28:7) 25 points

(16) What did Jesus do when the boat set sail? (Luke 8:23) 15 points

(17) When I am faced with a hard problem, how can Jesus help? Read Psalm 27:14. 20 points

(18) Timid Timothy is afraid to make new friends. How can Jesus help him? Read Psalm 30:10. 20 points

(19) "Behold, God is mine _____." (Psalm 54:4) 25 points

(20) "In thee, O Lord, do I put my _____ . . ." (Psalm 71:1) 25 points

(21) How did Jesus help the disciples when they were afraid? (Mark 4:39) 15 points

(22) What do you think Jesus says to us when we are afraid? Read Matthew 14:27. 20 points

(23) "But my _____ shall supply all your _____ according to his riches in glory by Christ Jesus." (Philippians 4:19) 25 points

(24) "Be of good courage, and he shall _____ your _____, all ye that hope in the Lord." (Psalm 31:24) 25 points

(25) "I will go in the _____ of the Lord _____." (Psalm 71:16) 25 points

(26) How did the disciples feel when they saw His power? (Luke 8:25) 15 points

(27) What can I do when I am afraid? Read Psalm 56:3. 20 points

(28) "The Lord is my _____ and my salvation; whom shall I _____?" (Psalm 27:1) 25 points

(29) "What time I am afraid, I _____ in thee." (Psalm 56:3) 25 points

(30) "Thou shalt _____ me with thy counsel." (Psalm 73:24) 25 points

WRITE-A-STORY

Any number of children

Subject: Facing a difficult situation

Bible learning objective: Learning Scriptures that help us make right choices in our lives.

Educational objective: Helping children choose acceptable behavioral patterns.

Evaluation procedure: Group discussion with peers.

Materials needed:
folder, magazine pictures, glue, paper, pencil

Directions:
1. Find pictures in a magazine of happy and unhappy faces of children. (Other folders might show a series of pictures depicting a problem for a young child.)
2. Glue these pictures inside the folder.

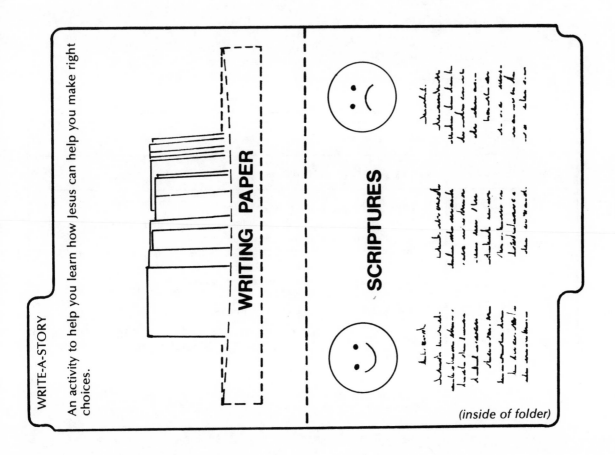

(inside of folder)

3. List appropriate Scriptures, from which the children may choose, that will guide them in finding solutions in God's Word.
4. Prepare the inside and outside of the folder as shown in the diagrams.
5. Provide a time during class when each child can share his or her story or cartoon.

Variation:

Duplicate the stories and cartoons. Each child can make a booklet of the class work.

Scriptures for folder:

Daniel 6:20-22	Matthew 25:38, 40
Joshua 1:9	Psalm 46:1
Philippians 4:19	Psalm 115:12
Psalm 145:18	Psalm 119:151
Psalm 27:1	2 Timothy 2:15
Psalm 32:7	Psalm 54:4
Luke 6:35	James 5:16
Psalm 146:9	Isaiah 41:6
Deuteronomy 10:19	Galatians 6:10
Psalm 30:10	1 John 4:7
Proverbs 17:17	Luke 6:22
James 1:17	Luke 6:31

WRITE-A-STORY

Who can use:	any number of children
You will need:	writing paper, pencils, Bibles
How to use:	1. Look at the pictures inside the folder. 2. Find a Scripture from those listed that might help the child solve his or her problem. 3. Write a story about the pictures. Be sure to tell how the child solved the problem by reading and applying God's Word. 4. Draw a cartoon to show what happened. *Pray without ceasing.* (1 Thessalonians 5:17)

(outside of folder)

TIDDLY-PONG

For two players or two teams

Subject: When I am afraid

Bible learning objective: Finding Scriptures that will help children face fearful situations

Educational objectives: Identifying fearful situations and developing positive behaviors to cope with them.

Evaluation procedure: Peer discussion.

Materials needed:

folder, poster board, Bible, two buttons, score paper, pencils, two pennies, felt

---

Directions:

1. Open the folder and transfer the game board. (You will need to make *two* game boards.)

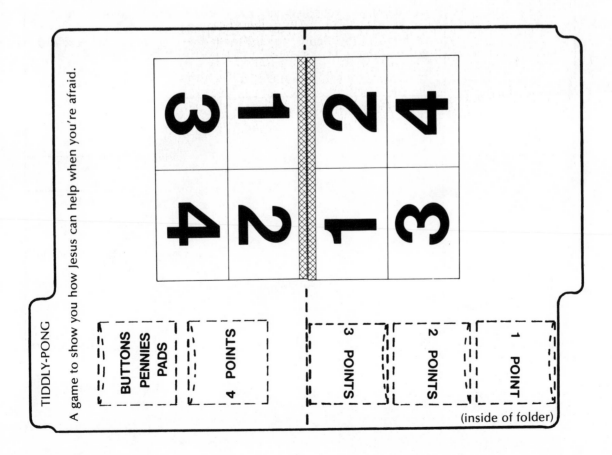

2. Tear out the pages and make twenty-seven discussion cards.
3. Glue the cards to the back side of the different colored poster board: red for pocket 1, blue for pocket 2, etc.
4. Make two felt pads, three by four inches.
5. Prepare the outside of the folder as shown in the diagram.

TIDDLY-PONG	
Who can play:	two children or two teams
You will need:	game board, Bible, pencil, score sheet, discussion cards, felt pads, two pennies, two buttons
How to play:	1. The first team or player will begin serving on square four. 2. Try to flip the button over the net by pressing it into the felt pad with a penny as in Tiddly Winks. 3. If the server doesn't get the button over the net in three serves, the serve passes to the next player. 4. A player must choose a card from the numbered pocket that matches the number in the court where his or her button lands. 5. Follow the directions on the card. You receive the same number of points as shown on the pocket for your score. 6. If you land on #4, you choose a card and fill in the blanks from memory for four points. If you have to look up the verse, you get only two points. 7. The winner is the first player or team to score 21 points. *Go home to thy friends, and tell them how great things the Lord hath done for thee.* (Mark 5:19) (outside of folder)

130

When Mark was a young child, a puppy nipped his heels while he was playing with it. Mark was too young to realize the puppy didn't mean to hurt him. As a result of this incident, he is terrified of dogs.

Mark walks home from school every day. He passes a yard in which a huge dog barks and lunges savagely at the fence. Mark is afraid.

Read Daniel 6:20-22 to the other players and explain how Mark can use these verses to help him when he is afraid.

pocket 1

Phil is beginning fourth grade in a new school. The teacher is friendly enough, but the children stare at him with questioning eyes. He wonders if his hair is sticking up in the back. He wonders if he'll be able to find the cafeteria. He even wonders if he'll be able to find his way home after school. Phil is afraid of being the new boy in a strange school.

Read Psalm 146:9 to the other players and explain how this verse could help Phil.

pocket 1

Jennifer has never been good at math. Just the word math or problem is enough to make her grit her teeth. Every Friday the teacher gives a test, and every Friday Jennifer's mouth is dry and her hands tremble as she writes her name on her paper. The butterflies in her stomach turn flipflops.

Jennifer is afraid to take tests. Read 2 Timothy 2:15 to the other players and explain how this verse could help her.

pocket 1

Mike begs his dad for a new trail bike. "All the other guys have them," he says. "The other kids make fun of you if you're still riding a baby bike." Mike's Dad doesn't approve of motor bikes for ten-year-olds, and Mike doesn't have the money to buy a ten-speed right now.

Mike is afraid of being different from the other kids. Read Luke 6:22 to the other players and explain how Mike can use this verse when he is afraid of being different.

pocket 1

"Blessed are ye, when men shall hate you, and when they shall separate you from their company, and shall reproach you, and cast out your name as evil, for the Son of man's sake" (Luke 6:22).

Tell about a time when you were afraid of being different from the rest of the gang even though you knew it was wrong to be like them.

How could the above verse help you the next time you know it is wrong to be like the rest of the kids?

pocket 2

"And there arose a great storm of wind, and the waves beat into the ship, so that it was now full. And he was in the hinder part of the ship, asleep on a pillow: and they awake him, and say unto him, Master, carest thou not that we perish? And he arose, and rebuked the wind, and said unto the sea, Peace, be still. And the wind ceased, and there was a great calm. And he said unto them, Why are ye so fearful?" (Mark 4:37-40).

Tell about a time when you were afraid of a storm. How will this verse help you next time?

pocket 2

". . . And the king spake and said to Daniel, O Daniel, servant of the living God, is thy God, whom thou servest continually, able to deliver thee from the lions? Then said Daniel unto the king . . . My God hath sent his angel, and hath shut the lions' mouths, that they have not hurt me: *for I am innocent before God*" (Daniel 6:20-22).

Tell of a time when you were afraid of an animal. How could the story of Daniel help you when you are afraid?

pocket 2

Mike is a friend of yours. He rides a beat-up bike. Many of the kids have ten-speeds or motor bikes. You hear the guys make fun of Mike's bike. A few days later, you notice Mike walking to school. You know he is ashamed to ride his bike. What can you do to help him?

Choose one of these verses to help you find a way:

1 John 4:7	James 5:16
Luke 6:35	Proverbs 17:17
Luke 6:22	James 1:17
	Luke 6:31

pocket 3

---

7. "And the king spake and said to _____, O Daniel, servant of the living God, is thy _____, whom thou servest continually, able to deliver thee from the _____? Then said Daniel unto the king . . . My _____ hath shut the lions' mouths, that they have not hurt me," *for I am innocent before God* (Daniel 6:20-22).

pocket 4

Discussion cards

Amy hears strange scratching noises outside her window. The shadows of familiar objects in her room grow into frightening monsters. Amy is afraid of the dark. Read Psalm 56:3 to the other players and explain how Amy can use this verse when she is afraid of the dark.

pocket 1

"What time I am afraid, I will trust in thee" (Psalm 56:3).

Tell the other players about a time when you were afraid of the dark.

How could this verse help you the next time you are afraid?

pocket 2

"The Lord preserveth the strangers" (Psalm 146:9).

What does preserve mean?

Tell of a time when you were a stranger in a strange place.

How could this verse help you?

pocket 2

Pam is your best friend. One day she tells you a secret: she is afraid to be left alone. She asks you to come to her house while her mother goes to the store. How can you help her?

Choose one of these verses to help you find a way:

Psalm 27:1   Psalm 115:13
Joshua 1:9   Psalm 56:3

pocket 3

---

4. "And he arose, and rebuked the wind, and said unto the sea, _____, _____ _____. And the wind ceased, and there was a great calm. And he said unto them, Why are ye so _____? how is it that ye have no faith?" (Mark 4:39, 40).

pocket 4

---

1. "Study to show thyself approved unto _____, a _____ that needeth not to be ashamed" (2 Timothy 2:15).

pocket 4

Lightning cracks outside Jeff's window. A few seconds later a loud boom of thunder shatters the still afternoon. Jeff squinches his eyes shut and claps his hands over his ears. Jeff is afraid of the storm.

Read Mark 4:37-40 to the other players and explain how this verse can help Jeff when he is afraid of a storm.

pocket 1

". . . and, lo, I am with you alway, even unto the end of the world" (Matthew 28:20).

How can this verse help you when you are alone? Tell the other players about a time when you were alone and scared.

pocket 2

You walk home from school every day with Mark. You own a large dog who is more bark than bite. Mark is terrified of your dog. What can you do to help?

Choose one of these verses to help you find a way:
Daniel 6:20-22   Joshua 1:9
Philippians 4:19   Psalm 145:18
Psalm 27:1

pocket 3

The teacher introduces a new boy named Phil to your class. He is dressed differently from the other kids. His hair sticks up in the back. He has a sick, scared look in his eyes. How can you help?

Choose one of these verses to help you find a way:
Psalm 146:9   Deuteronomy 10:19
Matthew 25:38-40

pocket 3

Jennifer sits across from you in math. She doesn't make very good grades. Every Friday she gets a stomachache during math class. You realize she is afraid she will fail. How can you help?

Choose one of these verses to help you find a way:
2 Timothy 2:15   Psalm 54:4
James 5:16   Isaiah 41:6
Galatians 6:10

pocket 3

Pam has been watching TV in the family room. She can hear the familiar sounds of water running and Mother's footsteps as she walks back and forth in the kitchen. Suddenly Pam stiffens and calls, "Mother?" There is no answer. Mother isn't there. Pam is afraid to be alone.

Read Matthew 28:20 to the other players and explain how Pam can use this verse to help her when she is afraid of being alone.

pocket 1

"Study to show thyself approved unto God, a workman that needeth not to be ashamed" (2 Timothy 2:15).

Tell about a time when you were afraid to take a test.

How can this verse help you the next time you are afraid to take a test?

pocket 2

A friend is spending the night with you. This friend tells you he sleeps with his light on at night because he is afraid of the dark. How can you help your friend?

Choose one of these verses to help you find a way:
Psalm 56:3   Psalm 30:10
Psalm 46:1   Psalm 27:1

pocket 3

---

5. "_____ are ye, when men shall hate you, and when they shall _____ you from their company, and shall reproach you, and cast out your name as evil, for the Son of man's sake" (Luke 6:22).

pocket 4

---

2. "The Lord preserveth the _____" (Psalm 146:9).

pocket 4

---

3. "And, lo, I am with _____ _____, even unto the end of the _____" (Matthew 28:20).

pocket 4

---

6. "What time I am _____, I will _____ in thee" (Psalm 56:3).

pocket 4

COMMANDMENTS FOR TODAY

For one to ten children

Subject: The Ten Commandments

Bible learning objective: Learning the Ten Commandments.

Educational objectives: Recognizing and developing acceptable behavioral patterns.

Evaluation procedure: Checking with the Bible and discussing with peers in a large group.

Materials needed:
folder, poster board, plastic tape, scissors, ruler, pencil

Directions:

These directions are for ten folders, one for each of the Commandments.

1. Open each of the ten folders and make a pocket chart on the inside as follows:

    a. From the poster board, cut 100 strips nine-and-a-half by three-fourths

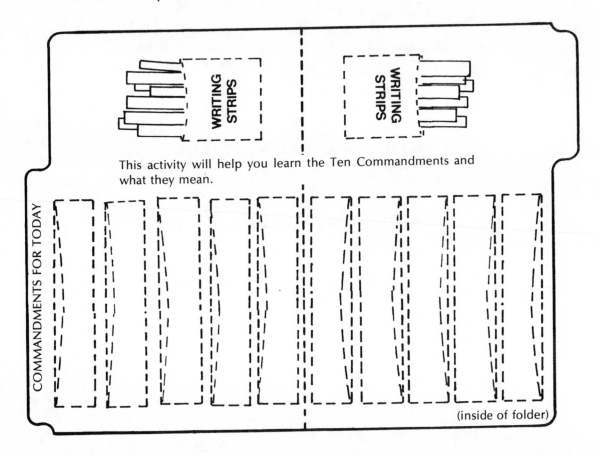

WRITING STRIPS

WRITING STRIPS

This activity will help you learn the Ten Commandments and what they mean.

COMMANDMENTS FOR TODAY

(inside of folder)

inches. You will need ten for each folder.

b. Mark lines every one-and-one-half inches on each side of the folder.

c. Place the poster board strip on the line and tape it on three sides so it forms a pocket. (Make sure the opening of the pocket is toward the top of the folder so the contents won't fall out when the folder is shut. This means the pockets face in different directions on each side. (See diagram.)

2. Write each of the Ten Commandments on a separate sentence strip and place one in the first pocket of each folder.

3. Prepare the outside of the folder as shown in the diagram.

4. Supply blank sentence strips, eight-and-a-half by three-fourths inches. Make a pocket three by six-and-a-half inches to hold them.

Extension:

Another use for the pocket chart folders is to hold cut apart Bible verses for the children to put in order. The variety for this activity is endless.

COMMANDMENTS FOR TODAY	
Who can use:	one to ten children
You will need:	sentence strips, pocket chart, Bible, pencil, dictionary
How to use:	1. Read the Commandment in the first pocket at the top of the chart. 2. Look up any words you do not know in the dictionary. 3. Get a sentence strip and rewrite the Scripture in today's language. Be careful not to change the meaning. 4. Read and compare your version of the Commandment with those already written by the other children. 5. Put your sentence strip in one of the empty pockets for others to read. (It is fun to use popular expressions, CB talk, and jive language when doing this exercise.) *O how I love thy law!* (Psalm 119:97) (outside of folder)

FISHING

For one child
Subject: The Ten Commandments
Bible learning objective: Learning the content of the Ten Commandments.
Educational objectives: Recognizing and developing acceptable behavioral patterns.
Evaluation procedure: Match work with Exodus 20.

Materials needed:
one and one-half folders, clear, plastic wrap, felt-tipped marker, string, Bible

Directions:
1. Open the folder and write the Ten Commandments, making the words wave up and down like water.
2. Write large, and omit some words. Leave a space the size of the fish pattern for each missing word.

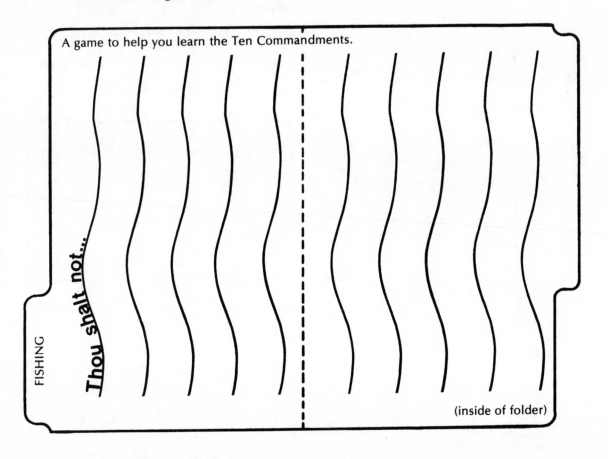

A game to help you learn the Ten Commandments.

FISHING

Thou shalt not...

(inside of folder)

3. Cut as many fish from tagboard as you have missing words, and tape a string in the mouth of each one.
4. Write a missing word on the tail of each fish.
5. Use the pattern and trace a fishbowl on the insertion folder.
6. Cut out the circle inside the bowl to make a window. Then cut a slit across the top of the bowl so the strings can hang out.
7. Tape a piece of plastic wrap over the back of the hole.
8. Cut a pocket six-and-a-half by seven inches from the tagboard.
9. Use plastic tape and attach the tagboard pocket on the other side of the insertion folder, over the plastic wrap. (See diagram.)
10. Place all the fish inside the pocket, with the strings hanging out of the bowl.
11. Prepare the outside of the folder as shown in the diagram.

FISHING	
Who can play:	one person
You will need:	Bible, fish
How to play:	1. Turn to Exodus 20 in your Bible. 2. Read the Commandments inside the folder and decide what words are missing. 3. Fish for each missing word by pulling on a string. 4. Place all of the fish on the Commandments to fill in the blanks. 5. Check your work with Exodus 20. *All that the Lord hath said will we do, and be obedient.* (Exodus 24:7) (outside of folder)

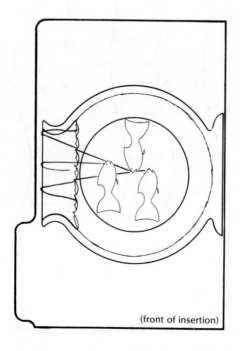

(front of insertion)

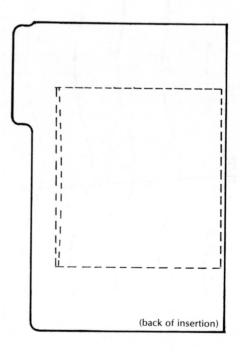

(back of insertion)

Cut slit

Trace this fishbowl on the insertion folder. Cut out the inner circle. Tape the plastic wrap on the other side over the hole. Tape a tag-board pocket, seven inches by six-and-one-half inches, over the plastic wrap. Cut a slit across the top of the fishbowl.

Fish

pattern

THE TOP TEN

For any number of children
Subject: The Ten Commandments
Bible learning objective: Practical applications of the Ten Commandments.
Educational objectives: Recognizing and developing acceptable behavioral patterns.
Evaluation procedure: Group discussion with peers.

Materials needed:
folder, construction paper, scissors, felt-tipped markers, Bible

Directions:
1. Prepare the outside and inside of the folder as shown in the diagrams.
2. Cut the records out of light-colored construction paper and type or print a problem on one side of each. Label the other side of the record, the flip side.

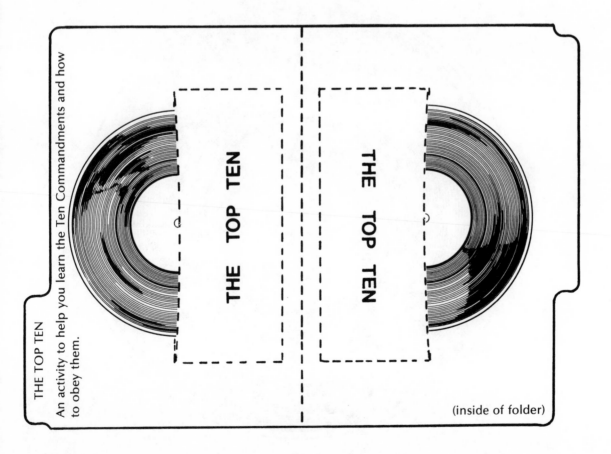

THE TOP TEN
An activity to help you learn the Ten Commandments and how to obey them.

THE TOP TEN

THE TOP TEN

(inside of folder)

THE TOP TEN

Who can use:	any number of children
You will need:	records, Bibles, pencils
How to use:	1. Open your Bible to Exodus 20. 2. Choose a record from "The Top Ten" pockets. 3. Read the problem on the record. Write below the problem what you think a person might do if he or she didn't know the Ten Commandments. 4. Turn the record over to the flip side and write the Commandment that applies to that situation. Draw a picture or write a paragraph telling how a person who does know about God's love might handle the same problem. 5. Share your work with the large group. *Thy word is true from the beginning.* (Psalm 119:160) (outside of folder)

Problem:

Record
pattern

Problems:

1. You are in a drugstore. You see a toy you have wanted for a long time. You just spent the last of your allowance on a chocolate bar. No one is looking. You. . .

2. Your mother tells you not to throw your football inside the house. She is gone to the grocery store. You begin to toss the ball in the air. It hits a lamp and knocks it to the floor. The lamp breaks. When Mother comes home, you . . .

3. It is a Sunday morning. You went to a late movie Saturday night. You are very sleepy. You . . .

4. Your friend received a new mini bike for his birthday. You want one, but your parents said you must wait until you are older. You . . .

5. You are with your friends at the swimming pool. You begin to wrestle. One of your friends becomes angry and calls you an ugly name. He uses God's name in an ugly way. You are angry, too. You . . .

6. Your mother tells you to empty the trash. You are watching TV. You know she is expecting company soon. You want to finish watching the program. You . . .

7. You are on the playground. You find a quarter in the dust. You . . .

8. Your dad told you to be home from a friend's house by 6:00 P.M. Your friend asks you to go with him to the skating rink. You know you won't be home by six. You . . .

9. One of your friends accuses you of cheating on a test. This makes you angry. You want to hurt your friend because he has hurt your feelings. You want to call him a dirty name. You . . .

10. A new boy in school hits you. You are angry with him. A few days later, the new boy himself is hit for no apparent reason. The teacher asks you who started the fight. You know you can get the new boy in trouble. You . . .

11. A friend invites you to go skiing. You know you will not be home in time to go to Sunday school. You . . .

12. It's your sister's birthday. Your own birthday isn't for several months. She gets a pair of roller skates. You would really like to have a pair, too. You . . .

PICK-A-WORD

For one player
Subject: The Ten Commandments
Bible learning objective: Applying the Ten Commandments.
Educational objective: Evaluation of behavioral patterns.
Evaluation procedure: Work is checked with Exodus 20.

Materials needed:
folder, construction paper, velcro, scissors, Bible, crayons or markers

Directions:
1. Open the folder and draw ten flowers inside. (Flower pattern is provided.) Color them with markers or crayons. (See diagram.)
2. Write the Ten Commandments on the flowers, but leave one word out of each. Also, be sure to leave the flower centers blank.

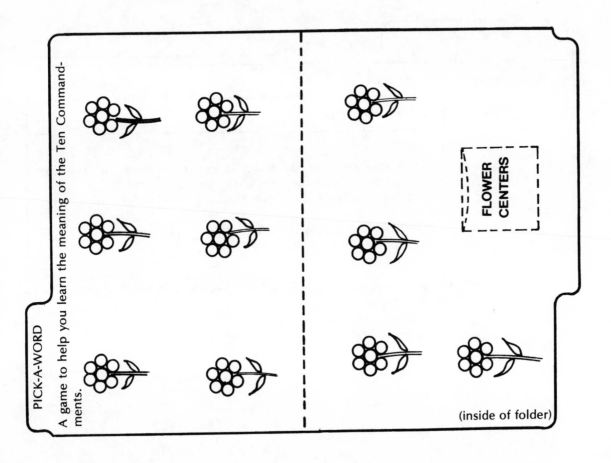

PICK-A-WORD

A game to help you learn the meaning of the Ten Commandments.

FLOWER CENTERS

(inside of folder)

3. Make ten circles from construction paper for the flower centers. Write the missing words on them.
4. Glue the velcro to the flower centers on the folders and to the backs of the construction paper circles.
5. Prepare the outside of the folder as shown in the diagram.

Suggestions for the wording of the Commandments on the flowers. The words in parentheses are for the center circles:

1. You must love _____ (God).
2. You must go to church on _____ (Sunday).
3. You must not _____ (kill).
4. You must tell the _____ (truth).
5. You must be _____ (happy) for your neighbor.
6. You must take only what is _____ (yours).
7. You must love your father and _____ (mother).
8. You must say sweet, loving _____ (words).
9. You must not _____ (commit) adultery.
10. You must worship only _____ (God).

PICK-A-WORD

Who can play:	one person
You will need:	flower centers, Bible
How to play:	1. Use the words on the flower centers to complete the Ten Commandments written on the flowers inside this folder. 2. When you finish, open your Bible and read Exodus 20. *If ye love me, keep my commandments.* (John 14:15)

(outside of folder)

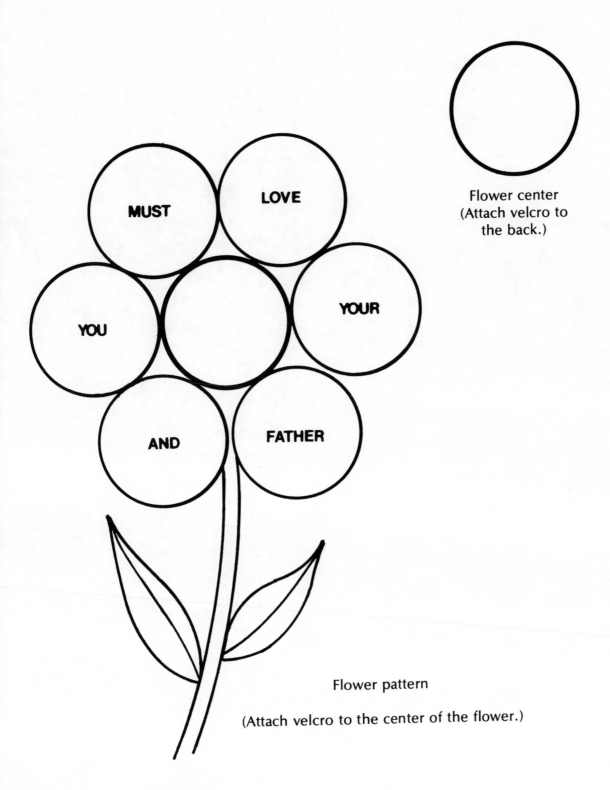

MUST

LOVE

YOU

YOUR

AND

FATHER

Flower center
(Attach velcro to
the back.)

Flower pattern

(Attach velcro to the center of the flower.)

LETTER FOLDER

For any number of children

Subjects: Letters to church members who are sick and absent . . . letters of appreciation to church workers

Bible learning objective: Involving the children in outreach activities toward fellow class members and church workers.

Educational objective: Encouraging written expression.

Evaluation procedure: Checking with the letter form on the folder for correct placement of the different letter parts.

Materials needed:
   one-and-one-half folders, blank paper, envelopes, pencils, Bible stickers, names and addresses of members and staff, fine-line magic markers, old greeting cards, old quarterlies

Directions:
1. Prepare the inside and outside of the folder as shown in the diagrams. The pockets will vary according to your individual needs as you may wish to in-

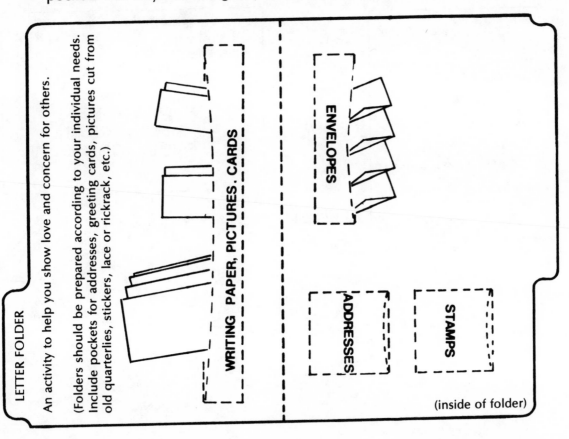

LETTER FOLDER

An activity to help you show love and concern for others.

(Folders should be prepared according to your individual needs. Include pockets for addresses, greeting cards, pictures cut from old quarterlies, stickers, lace or rickrack, etc.)

WRITING PAPER, PICTURES, CARDS

ENVELOPES

ADDRESSES

STAMPS

(inside of folder)

clude pockets for pieces of rickrack or lace.

2. Provide the necessary materials the children will need to complete their letters.

3. Prepare an insertion to the folder as shown.

LETTER FOLDER	
Who can use:	anyone
You will need:	paper, pencils, addresses, letter form (look on the insertion folder), felt-tipped markers, stickers, envelopes

How to use:	1. Choose a name from the list of addresses.
	2. Write a letter:
	  a. To the song leader, thanking him for bringing us good music.
	  b. To the minister, thanking him for being a good friend.
	  c. To an old person in church who might be lonely.
	  d. To someone who had a birthday this week.
	  e. To someone who has been absent from Sunday school.
	3. Check your letter with the letter form on the insertion folder.
	We are laborers together with God. (1 Corinthians 3:9)

(outside of folder)

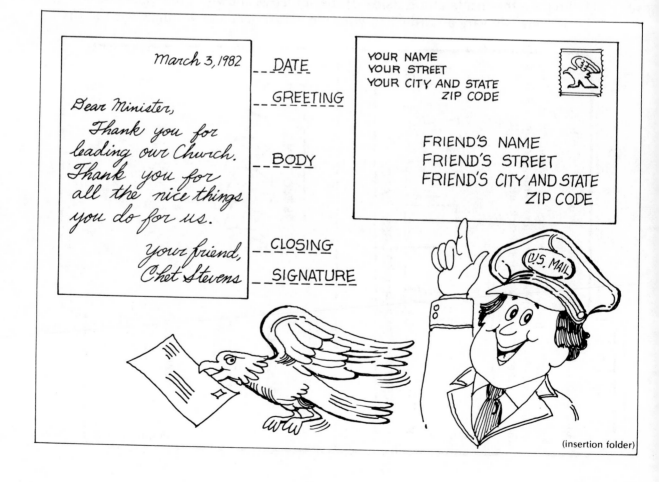

March 3, 1982 __ __DATE

__ __GREETING

Dear Minister,
  Thank you for leading our Church. Thank you for all the nice things you do for us.
      your friend,
      Chet Stevens

__BODY

__CLOSING

__ __SIGNATURE

YOUR NAME
YOUR STREET
YOUR CITY AND STATE
    ZIP CODE

FRIEND'S NAME
FRIEND'S STREET
FRIEND'S CITY AND STATE
      ZIP CODE

(insertion folder)

WHAT BUGS ME

For any number of children
Subject: Self-evaluation
Bible learning objective: Using the Word of God to help us deal with unpleasant situations.
Educational objective: Choosing acceptable behavioral patterns.
Evaluation procedure: Class discussion.

Materials needed:
   folder, construction paper, white paper, felt-tipped markers or crayons, pencils, Bible

---

Directions:
1. Open the folder and prepare the inside as shown in the diagram.
2. Cut the construction paper into four-by-six-inch rectangles.
3. Cut the white paper into strips one-half inch by three inches.

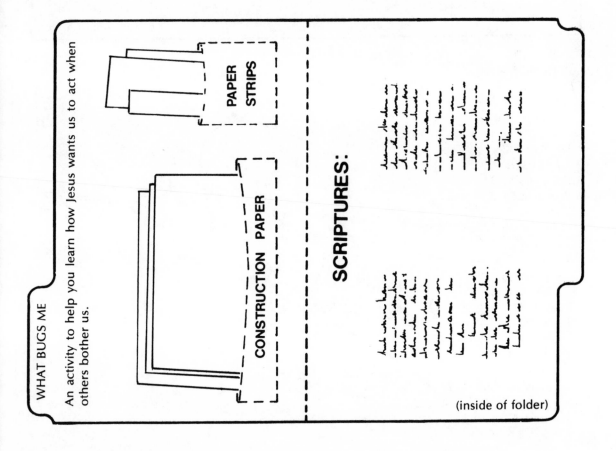

(inside of folder)

4. Write the Scriptures for the children to look up on one side of the folder.
5. Decorate the outside and inside of the folder with colorful pictures of bugs.
6. Glue the bug pattern to poster board to reinforce it before cutting it out.

WHAT BUGS ME	
Who can use:	anyone
You will need:	construction paper, strips of paper, Bible, crayons, markers, pencils, glue
How to use:	1. Draw a picture of a bug on the construction paper. Make it large. You can color the bug with crayons, or cut out parts for it from construction paper and glue them on. 2. Write something that bugs you or makes you angry on a strip of the white paper and glue it to one of the bug's wings. 3. Choose a verse of Scripture you will remember the next time something bugs you. Write it on a strip of paper and glue it to the other wing of your bug. *Blessed are they that hear the word of God, and keep it.* (Luke 11:28) (outside of folder)

Scriptures:

Ephesians 4:32
1 Corinthians 13:4-7
Luke 6:27
Romans 8:28
1 John 2:15
Proverbs 3:13
Proverbs 11:2
Luke 11:28
Ephesians 6:1
James 1:22
1 Peter 5:5
Hebrews 13:17
Matthew 18:21, 22
Luke 6:37
Psalm 84:11
Psalm 71:1
Psalm 37:1
Ephesians 6:13
2 Thessalonians 3:13
2 Timothy 2:15
James 3:17

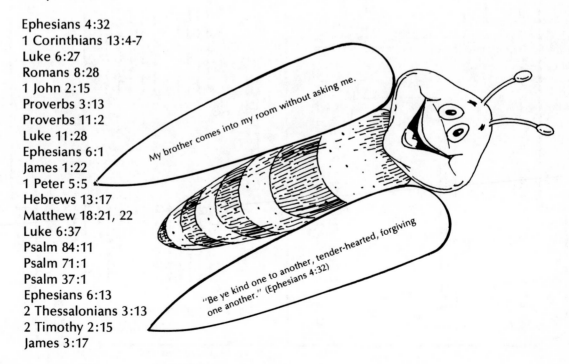

ᵒSES BLACKOUT

Amram and Jochebed
Made an ark of bulrushes and hid it in the river
Drawn out
A priest and his seven daughters
Miriam and Aaron
Pharaoh's daughter
80
Joshua and Caleb
Aaron
He was slow of speech.
Sang praises to God
They had to wander in the wilderness for 40 years.
Parted the Red Sea
Thou shalt have no other gods before me.
They were covered by the waters of the Red Sea.
Joshua
It was a land of giants.
A pillar of cloud by day and a pillar of fire by night
Ten Commandments
They worshiped the golden calf.
Joseph's bones
He broke them.
Going out
Mount Sinai

THE PROMISED LAND

Amram and Jochebed
Made an ark of bulrushes and hid him in the river
A priest and his seven daughters
A burning bush
They were slaves to the Pharaoh.
Lead the people out of Egypt
Going out
Waters turned to blood, frogs, lice, flies, boils, hail, locust, darkness, cattle died, firstborn babies died
Pillar of fire by night; pillar of cloud by day
Miriam
He was slow of speech.
Aaron
Parted the waters
They were covered by the waters.
Sang praises to God
Joseph's bones
Manna
Old Testament
Aaron
Mount Sinai
Ten Commandments
Worshiping the golden calf
"Thou shalt have no other gods before me."
A tabernacle
He broke them.
Joshua and Caleb
Aaron
They had to wander in the wilderness 40 years.
Joshua
120
It was a land of giants.
"All that the Lord hath said will we do, and be obedient."

1. Nile River
2. Led his flocks of sheep
3. No
4. Mount Nebo
5. He killed an Egyptian.
6. direct thy paths
7. and laid it in the river
8. Pharaoh's daughter
9. Jethro
10. in the sight of the Lord
11. drawn out
12. Miriam
13. than men
14. will we do, and be obedient

BIBLE FOOTBALL

Five-Yard Questions:
1. 12
2. A coat of many colors
3. Their father loved Joseph best.
4. To feed their father's flock
5. To check on his brothers
6. Kill him
7. Ishmaelites
8. Judah
9. They had found Joseph's coat.
10. Chief butler and chief baker
11. To tell Pharaoh that Joseph was innocent
12. No
13. Replace their money and put Joseph's silver cup in Benjamin's sack
14. Sent his sons to buy grain
15. Jacob wouldn't let Benjamin go.
16. He said they were spies.

Ten-Yard Questions:
1. The sheaves of Joseph's brothers bowed down to his sheaf.
2. The sun, moon, and stars bowed down to Joseph.
3. To throw Joseph into a pit
4. Twenty pieces of silver
5. Dipped it in a goat's blood
6. To Egypt
7. Potiphar's wife
8. He took grapes from a vine and crushed them into Pharaoh's cup.
9. He had three baskets of baked goods on his head. Birds ate from the top basket.
10. Seven fat cows were eaten by seven skinny cows.
11. Seven fat ears of grain were eaten by seven skinny ears of grain.
12. There would be seven prosperous years followed by seven years of famine.
13. To appoint a wise man to save grain during the good years to use during the famine
14. When his brothers came to buy grain, they bowed down to Joseph.
15. To put their money in their grain sacks
16. He ordered a meal to be prepared.
17. The land of Goshen

Twenty-Yard Questions:
1. In the land of Canaan
2. Do you really believe your mother, brothers, and I will bow down to you?

3. Dothan
4. Reuben
5. Potiphar
6. Placed him in charge of the prison
7. Joseph
8. Bring their brother Benjamin back to Egypt
9. Because of what they had done to Joseph
10. To return to Egypt with Benjamin and some gifts
11. He cried.
12. The person who took the cup would die and the others would become slaves.
13. Israel

Field-Goal Questions:
1. Sell Joseph to the Midianites
2. He would return to his old job in Pharaoh's house in three days.
3. In three days, he would die.
4. Sent for Joseph
5. 17
6. God
7. That Joseph had correctly interpreted his dream in prison
8. Joseph
9. He would bring Benjamin home safely.
10. God had sent him to Egypt to save lives.

Touchdown Questions:
1. gift, above
2. made, made, made
3. God, needs
4. hear, word, God
5. help, trouble
6. good, forgive
7. Lord, call
8. strength, afraid
9. Lord, commandments
10. teach, shalt go
11. God, helper
12. loved us, son
13. strong, afraid Lord
14. Lord, word, promise

Extra-Point Questions:
1. Genesis
2. The Nile
3. It was his birthday.
4. God would cause it to happen soon.
5. The Pharaoh's own ring
6. 30
7. Ephraim, Manasseh
8. Canaan
9. They thought Joseph would say they stole the money and make them slaves.
10. Because Egyptians hated the Hebrews and wouldn't eat with them

PENNY ROLL
1. He was the son of his old age.
2. The sheaves of his brothers and parents bowed down to Joseph's sheaf. The sun, moon, and eleven stars bowed down to Joseph.
3. Jacob rebuked Joseph.
4. 17
5. His father gave him a special coat. Joseph told on them when they disobeyed.

6. To kill him
7. Told on his brothers
8. To check on his brothers
9. It made them hate him.
10. Dothan
11. They had found Joseph's coat.
12. His house prospered.
13. The chief baker and chief butler
14. Reuben
15. Egypt
16. Potiphar's wife
17. He carried three baskets of baked goods on his head. Birds ate from the top basket.
18. Judah
19. He was sold as a slave.
20. Put Joseph in prison
21. He took grapes and crushed them into Pharaoh's cup
22. Dipped it in goat's blood
23. Potiphar
24. Placed him in charge of the prison
25. He would return to work in Pharaoh's house in th days.
26. He would be put to death in three days.
27. To interpret his dream
28. He felt that Joseph was wise.
29. To gather grain and store it for the years of famin
30. To tell Pharaoh about Joseph
31. God
32. 30
33. There were seven years of famine.
34. No
35. There would be seven good years and seven year famine.
36. Ephraim and Manasseh
37. Send his sons to Egypt to buy grain
38. Seven lean cows ate seven fat cows. Seven lean he of grain ate seven fat heads of grain.
39. To appoint a wise man to save grain for the year famine
40. He was afraid something would happen to him.
41. Ten of his sons
42. He accused them of being spies.
43. He wouldn't let Benjamin go to Egypt.
44. The person who had the cup would die and the r become slaves.
45. Bring Benjamin to Egypt
46. Benjamin and special gifts
47. Tore their clothes and returned to Egypt
48. His brothers bowed down to him.
49. Simeon
50. He invited them to dinner.
51. He told them who he was.
52. God, helper
53. Their money
54. Replace their money and put his silver cup in Be min's sack
55. Judah
56. me, truth, teach
57. Lord, good, forgive
58. refuge, trouble
59. thee
60. keep, places

JOSEPH WORD FIND
1. father
2. famine
3. kill

brothers
grain
pit
coat
dream
silver cup
Judah
Jacob
Judah
Egypt
Pharaoh
God
baker
butler

After you have found these answers in the Word Find, color Joseph's coat the way you imagine it looked.

NY SLIDE

Jesse

Philistines

Afraid

Go see about his brothers

Samuel

Nine feet

Eight

Left the sheep with a keeper

He had an evil spirit.

Goliath

Three

Riches and his daughter in marriage

Bread, wine, and a young goat

Send a man to fight with me

David

Why is this Philistine allowed to defy the armies of the living God?

He had come there to see the battle.

He had killed a lion and a bear.

He would give David's flesh to the birds and beasts.

His robe, sword, bow, and belt

Fight the Philistine giant

The Lord

I will defeat you and everyone will know there is a God in Israel.

Because the people were praising David more than they were Saul.

How can you fight him? You are just a boy.

God

He shot a stone from a sling and hit the giant in the forehead. Then David cut off his head.

He tried to kill him.

His armor

A sling and five smooth stones

31. Jonathan
32. To always be kind to each other and their children
33. He arranged a signal with arrows.
34. lifter up
35. love
36. courage, heart
37. Nob
38. godly, hear
39. words, heart
40. right, truth
41. Cut off the hem of Saul's robe
42. prayer
43. leadeth
44. refuge, strength, trouble
45. David took Saul's spear and water bottle while Saul slept.
46. trust, seek
47. teach, paths
48. our God, guide

MYSTERY MESSAGE

Mystery Words: share, love, salvation, truth
Mystery Word #1: love
Mystery Word #2: honest
Mystery Word #3: share

MYSTERY MESSAGE

1. Jericho
2. Tax collecting
3. He was too short.
4. Climbed a tree
5. Sycamore tree
6. To Zaccheus' house
7. Come down, Zaccheus, I'm going to your house to-day.
8. Jesus has gone to the house of a sinner.
9. Pay back four times the amount overcharged
10. Give half of his goods to the poor
11. Salvation has come to this house.
12. seek, save, lost

WHO AM I? TIC-TAC-TOE

1. Joseph	22. Isaac	43. Jacob
2. Joseph	23. Moses	44. Daniel
3. Isaac	24. Moses	45. Daniel
4. Joseph	25. Jacob	46. Abraham
5. Joseph	26. Moses	47. Daniel
6. Isaac	27. Jacob	48. Daniel
7. Isaac	28. Jacob	49. Abraham
8. Joseph	29. Moses	50. Abraham
9. Joseph	30. Moses	51. Daniel
10. Isaac	31. Jacob	52. Daniel
11. Joseph	32. Jacob	53. Abraham
12. Joseph	33. Moses	54. Abraham
13. Isaac	34. Moses	55. David
14. Isaac	35. Jacob	56. David
15. Joseph	36. Daniel	57. Elijah
16. Joseph	37. Daniel	58. Abraham
17. Isaac	38. Abraham	59. David
18. Isaac	39. Jacob	60. David
19. Moses	40. Daniel	61. Elijah
20. Moses	41. Daniel	62. Abraham
21. Jacob	42. Abraham	63. David

64. David
65. Elijah
66. Abraham
67. David
68. David
69. Elijah
70. David
71. David
72. Elijah
73. Elijah
74. Samson
75. Elijah
76. Samson
77. Elijah
78. Samson
79. Elijah
80. Samson
81. Elijah
82. Samson
83. Samson
84. Paul
85. Paul

86. Samson
87. Paul
88. Paul
89. Paul
90. Samson
91. Paul
92. Paul
93. Peter
94. Samson
95. Paul
96. Paul
97. Peter
98. Samson
99. Paul
100. Paul
101. Peter
102. Peter
103. Peter
104. Peter
105. Peter
106. Peter
107. Peter
108. Peter

BIBLE COVER-UP

Game board #1	Game board #2	Game board #3
1. David	1. Joseph	1. Paul
2. Elijah	2. Isaac	2. Paul
3. Elijah	3. Isaac	3. Peter
4. Daniel	4. Moses	4. Barnabas
5. Abraham	5. Jacob	5. Samson
6. Daniel	6. Moses	6. Barnabas
7. Abraham	7. Jacob	7. Barnabas
8. Abraham	8. Joseph	8. Samson
9. David	9. Joseph	9. Paul
10. Elijah	10. Isaac	10. Paul
11. Elijah	11. Joseph	11. Peter
12. David	12. Joseph	12. Peter
13. Daniel	13. Isaac	13. Samson
14. Abraham	14. Isaac	14. Barnabas
15. Abraham	15. Jacob	15. Paul
16. Abraham	16. Jacob	16. Barnabas
17. Daniel	17. Moses	17. Samson
18. Daniel	18. Moses	18. Paul
19. David	19. Jacob	19. Peter
20. Elijah	20. Moses	20. Peter
21. David	21. Jacob	21. Peter
22. Elijah	22. Moses	22. Paul
23. David	23. Isaac	23. Samson
24. David	24. Jacob	24. Paul
25. Daniel	25. Moses	25. Samson

PUZZLES

Word Find:
1. love
2. ill
3. worketh
4. neighbor
5. his
6. no
7. to
   love, ill, worketh, neighbor, his, no, to
   Love worketh no ill to his neighbor.

8. Love his neighbor as himself.
9. Jesus

ACROSTIC

1. Philippians
2. Hebrews
3. Galatians
4. 1 Thessalonians
5. 2 Thessalonians
6. 2 Corinthians
7. Romans
8. 1 Corinthians
9. 1 and 2 Timothy
10. Ephesians
11. Colossians
12. Titus
13. Philemon

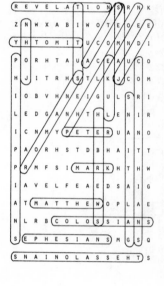

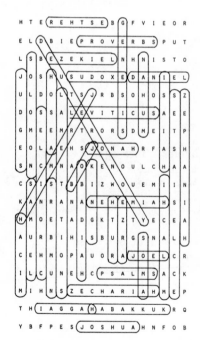

JERUSALEM TO JERICHO

1. Love the Lord with all thy heart
2. Passed by on the other side
3. A Samaritan
4. A lawyer
5. Which of these was a neighbor to the victim?

Jerusalem
Take care of him and I'll pay you back
A Levite
Go and do likewise
heart, soul, neighbor
Stopped to help the man
He was beaten.
Bound up his wounds and took him to an inn
A priest
Who is my neighbor?

ATTITUDES

signs on the hives should read:
ign #1
ign #2
ign #3
ign #4
ign #5
ign #6
ign #7
ign #8

ATTITUDES WORK SHEET:

I. 1. poor in spirit
   2. humble
   3. proud
   4. proud
   5. sin
   6. sin
II. 1. mourn
   2. sad, sorrow
   3. repent
   4. to be sorry about something, to change one's mind
   5. are sorry for their sins
III. 1. meek
   2. depend, God
   3. depend, God
. 1. hunger, thirst, righteousness
   2. just, good
   3. thoughts, right
   4. clean thoughts and right desires
. 1. merciful
   2. love
   3. kind, tender-hearted, forgiving
   4. kind, tender-hearted, forgiving
. 1. pure in heart
   2. love, love, good
   3. love
   4. love
. 1. peacemakers
   2. fight
   3. quarrel
   4. fight, quarrel
. 1. persecuted, righteousness'
   2. good
   3. mean, cruel
   4. mean, cruel

LL THE WATERS

Waves beat upon the ship.
There was a great calm.
A storm came up.
Water was filling the ship.

5. Ye have no faith.
6. The disciples
7. Go across the lake
8. Master, carest thou not that we perish?
9. His disciples
10. By the seaside
11. What manner of man is this?
12. (Read Psalm 31:24)
13. fear
14. strength, help
15. helped
16. He fell asleep.
17. He shall strengthen thine heart.
18. Lord, be thou my helper.
19. helper
20. trust
21. Stopped the storm
22. It is I, Be not afraid.
23. God, need
24. strengthen, heart
25. strength, God
26. afraid
27. Trust in God
28. light, fear
29. will trust
30. guide

TIDDLY-PONG

Cards for # four pocket:
1. God, workman
2. strangers
3. you, alway, world
4. peace, be still, fearful
5. blessed, separate
6. afraid, trust
7. Daniel, God, lions, God

THE TOP TEN

1. Thou shalt not steal.
2. Thou shalt not bear false witness against thy neighbor.
3. Remember the sabbath day, to keep it holy.
4. Thou shalt not covet.
5. Thou shalt not take the name of the Lord thy God in vain.
6. Honor thy father and thy mother.
7. Thou shalt not steal.
8. Honor thy father and thy mother.
9. Thou shalt not take the name of the Lord thy God in vain.
10. Thou shalt not bear false witness against thy neighbor.
11. Thou shalt have no other gods before me.
12. Thou shalt not covet.

PICK-A-WORD

1. God
2. Sunday
3. kill
4. truth
5. happy
6. yours
7. mother
8. words
9. commit
10. God

159